Columbia University

Contributions to Education

Teachers College Series

No. 581

AMS PRESS
NEW YORK

SOME CODE CONTROLS OF SCHOOL BUILDING CONSTRUCTION IN AMERICAN CITIES

AN EVALUATION OF CERTAIN BUILDING CODE REQUIREMENTS ESPECIALLY AS THEY INFLUENCE THE SAFETY OF THE OCCUPANTS, THE COST OF CONSTRUCTION, AND THE EDUCATIONAL EFFICIENCY OF THE SCHOOL BUILDING

WITH

CRITICISMS ON THE FORM AND METHOD OF MUNICIPAL BUILDING LEGISLATION

BY

JOHN W. SAHLSTROM, PH.D.

Teachers College, Columbia University Contributions to Education, No. 581

Published with the Approval of Professor N. L. Engelhardt, Sponsor

BUREAU OF PUBLICATIONS
TEACHERS COLLEGE, COLUMBIA UNIVERSITY
NEW YORK CITY
1933

Library of Congress Cataloging in Publication Data

Sahlstrom, John Wesley, 1894-
Some code controls of school building construction in American cities.

Reprint of the 1933 ed., issued in series: Teachers College, Columbia University. Contributions to education, no. 581.
Originally presented as the author's thesis, Columbia.
Bibliography: p.
1. School buildings--Law and legislation--United States. I. Title. II. Series: Columbia University. Teachers College. Contributions to education, no. 581.
KF5702.S3S2 1972 343'.73'078 70-177222
ISBN 0-404-55581-0

Reprinted by Special Arrangement with Teachers College Press, New York, New York

From the edition of 1933, New York
First AMS edition published in 1972
Manufactured in the United States

AMS PRESS, INC.
NEW YORK, N. Y. 10003

ACKNOWLEDGMENTS

GRATEFUL acknowledgment is made of the advice and encouragement given by Professor N. L. Engelhardt, the sponsor of this study, and Professor George D. Strayer and Professor J. R. McGaughy. Sincere appreciation is expressed for the cooperation of Mr. Clinton T. Bissell and his associates of the National Board of Fire Underwriters. The writer is indebted to his wife, Edith Irene Sahlstrom, for sympathetic counsel throughout the progress of the study.

J. W. S.

CONTENTS

TABLES AND CHARTS

TABLES

CHARTS

SOME CODE CONTROLS OF SCHOOL BUILDING CONSTRUCTION IN AMERICAN CITIES

CHAPTER I

INTRODUCTION

THE METHODS AND SCOPE OF THE STUDY

NUMEROUS exhaustive research studies and surveys have been made of the status, cost, and adaptability of the physical facilities provided for the housing of the educational program. These investigations have been concerned chiefly with those manifestations of construction which had a clear and immediate relationship to the educational activity. Other and less frequent inquiries have been projected recently into that sphere of school building operations in which the profession of school business administration has but recently recognized its responsibility. The technical and semi-technical phases of preparing specifications and working drawings preparatory to the construction of a school were formerly assumed to be the sole task of technicians in the related fields of architecture and engineering. The supervision of building operations, the duties and responsibilities of architects, contractors, and subcontractors—these and other similar aspects were but imperfectly understood by the average school official. There was, to be sure, the necessity of selecting the architect, but once he was selected, the tendency was to lodge in him a relatively single responsibility, especially with regard to the technical aspects of the job. This practice did not yield uniformly satisfactory results and there thus came to be a gradual acceptance by the educational profession of a share, although a minor one, in the technical phases of schoolhouse construction. The past few years have witnessed the appearance of a few notable investigations [1] which seem to be in whole or in part a response to the need of a wider participation of school officials in the planning and construction of schools.

[1] Lee Byrne, *Check List Materials for Public School Building Specifications Covering the General Specifications.*

A. M. Proctor, *Safeguarding the School Board's Purchase of Architects' Working Drawings.*

George D. Strayer and N. L. Engelhardt, *School Building Problems.*

G. F. Womrath, *Efficient Business Administration of Public Schools.*

The present study, an investigation of the effects of municipal building codes upon the construction of schools, relates the peculiar needs of the school to regulations of a more or less technical character. It does not purport, however, to be concerned with the problems of pure or applied engineering or architecture. In a sense it is an extension of those investigations which are designed to enable the responsible school official to plan, supervise, and finance building operations on a more scientific basis.

No extensive or organized body of evidence has ever been assembled to show the influence of municipal building ordinances upon the safe, efficient, and economical construction of schools. Neither does there appear to be a precedent to this study with respect to other types of buildings. True, there have been isolated and fragmentary reports on this subject in trade and professional journals, but most of them have been founded upon opinion and speculation.

The problem suggested itself while the writer was working with Professors George D. Strayer and N. L. Engelhardt of Teachers College, Columbia University, in reviewing proposed plans for school buildings. Issues were raised with architects on certain building features which seemed to the reviewer to serve no useful purpose, but increased construction costs. To be sure, the architect was fully aware of the situation, but in many instances he was compelled by local building legislation to include the unnecessary provision regardless of cost. A stimulus was thereby given to an interest in a subject which finally developed into an extensive investigation.

Through the courtesy of the National Board of Fire Underwriters, a rather large collection of city building codes from all parts of the country was made available for study. The study began in a tentative way, the purpose being to gain familiarity with a legal instrument whose terminology, form, and content were wholly foreign to the writer's experience. Through conferences with numerous code writers and building officials, a working knowledge was acquired which appeared sufficient for the proper interpretation of code requirements.

From the very first, serious difficulties were encountered. Codes were found that were completely lacking in either index or table of contents, and others contained conflicting provisions in different sections without cross references to guard against error.

Requirements were frequently written in a style which effectively concealed the intent of the law, and in many instances sections relating to an individual subject were scattered throughout several chapters. All reasonable care was taken to overcome these difficulties to the end that the true intent of the building code might be discovered. No attempt was made at any time to secure the interpretation of the building officials of the several cities from which the codes were taken. Such a procedure would have involved the use of a questionnaire which would have approximated in size and content some of the smaller codes. The results obtained by a direct reading of the building codes were useful in an additional way. A measure of the clarity of requirements, as written in some of the codes, was secured.

One hundred building codes from cities of various sizes located in the several geographical sections of the United States were selected for study. Since it was desired to secure average practice, the question of the date of the code was disregarded, the only precaution taken being the assurance that the code had not been superseded by a later edition. The date of promulgation and adoption of these codes ranged from 1915 to 1932. Each code was checked against a mimeographed tabulation of a survey made in July 1931 by the Building Code Committee of the United States Bureau of Standards, to make certain that it was effectively in force.

The sampling of cities was conditioned to a considerable extent by the availability of their effective codes. Numerous trials were made before the final list was completed. In many instances an attempt was made to secure codes directly from the building bureaus of the cities. In a few cases this procedure brought results, but more often the request was disregarded or the information volunteered that the code was in process of revision, or that there was only a limited number of copies left and they were not for distribution. The final list comprised a grouping as follows:

Distribution of Cities According to 1930 United States Census	*Number of Cities*
0– 10,000	3
10,000– 50,000	34
50,000–100,000	29
100,000–500,000	30
Over 500,000	4
TOTAL	100

Geographical Distribution of Cities	*Number of Cities*
New England States	13
Middle Atlantic States	7
East North Central States	18
West North Central States	11
South Atlantic States	17
East South Central States	7
West South Central States	11
Mountain States	7
Pacific States	9
TOTAL	100

Detailed analysis of the code requirements of cities according to geographical distribution was abandoned after it was made certain that no significant variations were likely to develop. Although there is a tendency for smaller cities to copy or adapt the codes of larger neighboring cities, there does not seem to be a general factor of localization. Codes originating on the West coast are found reproduced in New England cities, and the reverse is also true. A tabular analysis in the early part of the study confirmed the belief that the problem was regional rather than local. The selection of cities according to size was naturally limited to a relatively few on the upper and lower population levels.

This study does not at any point attempt to analyze the extent to which written provisions are incorporated in the actual construction of schools. It is confined to a critical evaluation of the printed code. In conference with building officials in a number of cities, however, it was discovered incidentally that practice in the use of administrative discretion varied to a great extent. Thus, while the building official holding office at the time of the conference conceived the code as rather flexible, his predecessor had held the opposite view, or the contrary might have been true. Apparently there have been all degrees of interpretation and application, ranging from the most rigid to the most lenient.

In the early stages of the study the intent was to investigate in considerable detail a large number of different school building requirements. Thus, there was built up a body of tabular material and other data on approximately twenty-five separate structural elements. The advice of competent authority and the experience gained in the progress of the study convinced the writer that the inclusion of so many items would seriously limit the number of building codes which could be studied. Furthermore, it was discovered that such an extensive investigation would necessarily be restricted to a mere reporting and explanation of numerous requirements, to the almost total exclusion of any thoughtful consideration of the adequacy of, or sound bases for, these requirements. Finally, it was revealed during the course of the investigation that the assumptions inherent in the form or arrangement of building codes were in large measure responsible for variations and inappropriateness of requirements. Thus, the plan, so commonly followed, of governing building construction by large, general, inclusive requirements without particular regard for individual needs of single types of buildings defeated, to a significant extent, the beneficial effects of regulation.

The choice, then, was between continuing the original plan of the study, which included relatively few cities and a large number of different building requirements, with resulting limitations, and abandoning the above plan in favor of a critical and searching review of current methods of controlling construction with a significantly large representation of cities and a reduction in the number of specific items consistent with the needs of sampling and the time and space available. The latter plan appeared to offer an infinitely more significant opportunity, since it partook of the advantages of the former plan and, in addition, treated the data in such a way that they disclosed in a positive manner the fallacies of generally accepted methods of control. It seemed to strike at the very root of the difficulties, the inadequacies and wasteful effects of municipal building legislation as now constituted.

The latter plan was adopted and the materials of the former plan were discarded. Chapters I and II are rather intimately concerned with a general discussion and argument on the subject of general versus individual control of building operations. Chapters III and IV show specifically how various methods of control have influenced the requirements for the schools.

As was to be expected, many incidental and desirable developments resulted at various stages of the study. These have been duly noted in relation to their significance and the space available.

SCOPE AND AUTHORITY OF BUILDING LAWS

The building code is a compilation of the laws and ordinances which provide legal minimum standards for materials and methods in the erection, removal, demolition, or alteration of all buildings within the area of jurisdiction. It regulates the use and occupancy of buildings, and prescribes permissible locations for various types of buildings within the fire districts. Requirements with reference to maintenance and equipment, insofar as these elements affect the public safety, are included. The code provides for a system of inspection, approval of plans, the issuance of permits, the collection of fees, and penalties for violations.

STATE AND LOCAL BUILDING LAWS

In its most recent and comprehensive form, the building code has been initiated, developed, adopted, and administered under the direction of municipal authorities. The delegation of legislative powers by the state to its political subdivisions, the city and the county, has not, however, eliminated the state from rather active participation in the control of building construction. State departments of labor, sanitation, health, and education exercise varying degrees of supervision over building operations within their spheres of authority. The consequent division of authority among the different departments of the state and city governments presents a situation that is needlessly complicated and cumbersome. Often the laws are so obscure that it is not quite clear in which authority enforcement of a given section is lodged. Sometimes there is concurrent jurisdiction. In 1920 Hart[2] reported nineteen states in which control of school building construction was vested in two or more different state agencies. McGowan's[3] analysis of state school building codes in 1929 showed that in the thirty-four states requiring submission of plans there were ten different organizations charged with the authority to inspect and to grant approval. In some instances plans had to be submitted to as many as four different departments or agencies within the same state. His analysis revealed a great divergence between the scope of requirements in the different states, some of which were detailed and exacting while others were scarcely beyond the stage of suggestion.

Local building codes, generally applicable to municipal areas,

[2] Frank W. Hart, *A Standard State Schoolhousing Code*, p. 9.

[3] H. M. McGowan, "An Analysis of State School Building Codes," *Educational Research Bulletin*, Vol. X, No. 17, p. 461, November 1931. College of Education, The Ohio State University.

are in a few instances either duplications or extensions of the state code. This is especially true where the state has a highly developed code. When the state has given little or no attention to this problem, the local code has become the major legal safeguard against incompetent and dangerous construction. Considering the fact that only a few states have comprehensive schoolhousing laws or regulations, it is evident that building activity is carried on without legal supervision in many communities. In 1921 there were 450 cities of populations from 10,000 to 25,000 that had no standardized building requirements, and at least 65 per cent of these cities had no building codes whatsoever.[4] Of 300 cities with populations in excess of 25,000, one-fourth had no building codes. In the absence of local codes these cities resorted to state regulations, underwriters' codes, or decisions and judgments of special groups of municipal authorities.

Table 1, a summary of an investigation made by the Building Code Committee of the United States Bureau of Standards in 1931, shows that 500 of the cities with population of over 5,000, had no local building ordinances. True reports on the cities that failed to respond to the Committee's inquiry would probably add materially to this number. It is possible to make only a rough estimate as to how many of these five hundred or more cities are located in states that have no adequate schoolhousing laws. McGowan's [5] study shows that the greatest variation exists in the requirements made by the various states with reference to those structural features which are major factors in fire protection. McGowan reported that thirty-three states had no statutory requirements on permissible heights of school buildings, elevations of first floors above grade, widths of stairways and corridors, floor construction, and materials for wall construction. If the absence of these statutory requirements constitutes inadequate regulation, then 247 of the 500 cities have neither local nor adequate state school building laws. Other cities, regardless of the presence or absence of a state code, have promulgated ordinances of their own. This procedure usually finds legal sanction in the state code, as indicated in the following sentence.

[4] George H. Dacy, "Why Not a Nation-Wide Building Code?" *Scientific American*, pp. 42–43, November 1921.

[5] H. M. McGowan, *An Analysis of State School Building Codes of the United States*, Table 7, p. 20. Unpublished doctor's dissertation, The Ohio State University, 1929.

TABLE 1

NUMBER OF CITIES WITH POPULATIONS OVER 5,000 WITH AND WITHOUT BUILDING CODES, THE DATE OF CODES, AND THE NUMBER OF CODES BEING REVISED *

STATES	NUMBER OF CITIES WITH NO CODES	NUMBER OF CITIES NOT REPORTING	NUMBER OF CITIES USING STATE CODE	NUMBER OF CITIES REVISING CODES	NUMBER OF CITIES WITH CODES	DATE OF CODE				TOTAL CITIES
						1921 TO 1931	1911 TO 1920	1901 TO 1910	BEFORE 1901	
Alabama	3	6	0	4	13	11	2			22
Arizona	2	1	0	3	6	3	2	1		9
Arkansas†	2	8	0	0	8	5	2		1	18
California	7	6	0	10	82	73	7	2		95
Colorado†	2	2	0	1	14	8	2	4		18
Connecticut	14	0	0	3	29	18	10		1	43
Delaware	0	0	0	0	1			1		1
Florida†	3	7	0	4	22	18	4			32
Georgia	5	7	0	1	20	14	5	1		32
Idaho	4	0	0	0	5	3	1		1	9
Illinois	30	18	0	13	69	42	19	7	1	117
Indiana	28	9	1	4	23	14	6	3		61
Iowa	16	1	0	4	19	15	3	1		36
Kansas	6	4	0	1	22	20	2			32
Kentucky	8	8	0	0	13	9	4			29
Louisiana	3	6	0	1	10	9			1	19
Maine†	7	0	1	0	14	6	7	1		22
Maryland	2	1	0	1	6	6				9
Massachusetts	35	4	0	13	78	49	26	3		117
Michigan†	23	8	2	6	42	30	10	2		75
Minnesota	11	3	0	4	18	8	6	1	3	32
Mississippi	4	3	0	1	10	6	3	1		17
Missouri	5	7	0	3	25	20	3	2		37
Montana	0	0	0	3	12	1	9	2		12
Nebraska	9	1	0	4	7	4	2	1		17
Nevada	0	0	0	0	2	2				2
New Hampshire	7	1	0	1	6	5	1			14
New Jersey	12	12	0	14	92	64	23	5		116
New Mexico	0	2	0	1	5	3	1	1		7
New York	22	6	0	15	85	62	18	3	2	113
North Carolina	2	5	11	4	20	18	1	1		38
North Dakota	2	0	0	0	8	5	1	2		10
Ohio	51	10	6	3	45	30	13	2		112
Oklahoma	10	8	0	0	22	17	4	1		40
Oregon	4	0	0	2	11	10	1			15
Pennsylvania	103	26	1	9	72	44	16	9	3	202
Rhode Island	3	1	0	1	16	14	2			20
South Carolina	3	5	1	3	11	5	6			20
South Dakota	1	1	0	0	6	4	2			8
Tennessee	3	4	0	1	14	8	4	2		21
Texas	19	16	0	3	52	39	11	1	1	87
Utah	0	1	0	2	6	4	2			7
Vermont	5	2	0	1	4	3			1	11
Virginia	6	4	0	4	16	12	3	1		26
Washington	3	0	0	4	16	11	2	3		19
West Virginia	4	4	0	3	14	11	3			22
Wisconsin	11	1	4	7	31	21	10			47
Wyoming	0	1	0	1	4	2	1	1		5
Total	500	220	27	163	1,126	786	260	65	15	1,873

* Data arranged from a questionnaire study by the U. S. Bureau of Standards, Division of Building and Housing, Washington, D. C., July, 1931.

† Cities reporting "Fire Limits" only were considered as having no code.

This code shall not limit the power of cities, villages, and towns to make, or enforce, additional or more stringent regulations, provided the same do not conflict with this code or with any order of the Industrial Commission.[6]

It is at once apparent from this discussion that many districts are subject to exacting requirements, while others are compelled to rely upon the competence and integrity of architects and contractors, with the possibility of a quasi-control by some branch of the local government. The issue is extended to rural and consolidated school districts where construction activities are carried on without any municipal jurisdiction and only meagre state supervision. Determination of the status of schoolhousing in these communities, with reference to those elements within the province of the building code, constitutes a major problem in itself.

The preparation of a building code is extremely complex, requiring the services of technicians highly skilled in the building arts and thoroughly conversant with the compilation of legal acts applying thereto. The proposed code for the City of New York [7] was completed in 1931 after three years of work. It involved the combined services of 125 specialists and the expenditure of more than $50,000. The scope and character of the requirements in large urban centers obviously exceed the range and type of regulation needed in smaller cities. The cost and quality of the service required in the preparation of codes for smaller cities, however, do not diminish proportionately as the size of the city decreases. The smaller community, limited as to budget and expert service, is confronted with a situation which has been met in various ways. Frequently there appears to have been a complete or modified adoption of the code from a larger neighboring city. Thus the New York City code has been the model for several other codes in the East. The small city codes in the Middle West show to a marked degree the influence of the Chicago and Minneapolis codes. Underwriters' codes and the codes prepared by special organizations, notably the Pacific Coast Building Officials Conference, are being used to an increasing degree. Manufacturing and commercial enterprises interested in the building trades have provided localities with regulations. Recently, the commendable work done by the United States Bureau of Standards has become the basis for code production.

[6] *Wisconsin State Building Code*, p. 9, 1931.
[7] *New York Times*, January 15, 1932.

There are no data on the exact extent to which small cities appropriate other codes or prepare their own. It is certain, however, that both procedures are followed in current practice, and it seems equally certain that neither local promulgation nor adoption of existing codes is entirely practical for the small city. The smaller city, in adopting the metropolitan code, must omit or make substitution for those provisions (and they are numerous) which involve the functions of a technical administrative staff, the facilities for testing materials and processes, and the machinery for constant revision. The codes prepared by underwriters and by building officials groups are definitely planned to meet the needs of widely diversified communities. Even in these instruments, however, assumptions are made that there will be local facilities for the determination of acceptable uses of alternate methods and materials of construction.

> The Building Inspector may approve such alternate types of construction or materials and may recommend an amendment to this Code in order to make permissible the use of same. If the evidence and proof are not sufficient, in the opinion of the Building Inspector, to justify approval or recommendation for an amendment, the applicant may refer the entire matter to the Board of Examiners and Appeals as specified in Section ———.[8]

It is not certain that the city below 25,000 in population will be able to command the services of inspectors or boards of appeals who can make the discriminations that are essential in securing substantial justice, safety, and economy.

> In order to determine the suitability of alternate materials and construction and to provide for reasonable interpretations of the provisions of this Code, there shall be and is hereby created a Board of Examiners and Appeals, consisting of five (5) members, who are qualified by experience and training to pass on matters pertaining to building construction. One member shall be a practicing architect, one a competent builder, one a lawyer, and two structural engineers, each of whom shall have had at least ten years' experience as an architect, builder, lawyer or structural engineer. The Building Inspector shall be an ex-officio member and shall act as Secretary to the Board. The Board of Examiners and Appeals shall be appointed. . . .[9]

The initial revision of a general code to fit a local situation can be accomplished, but there is no obligation on the part of the agencies promulgating the parent code to keep the local code up to date. And local authorities are not under any legal compulsion

[8] Pacific Coast Building Officials Conference, *Uniform Building Code*, p. 9, 1930.
[9] *Ibid.*, p. 10.

to amend, repeal, or add provisions in harmony with the rapid advance in the building industry, except as directed by a limited number of state codes. Continued and voluntary revision in the smaller city is probably rare, and is restricted to localities where energetic and public-spirited administration is available. In the tabulation by the United States Bureau of Standards the following situation was revealed:

16 cities have codes 30 years old or older;
64 cities have codes 20 to 30 years old;
260 cities have codes 10 to 20 years old; and
786 cities have codes less than 10 years old.

The age at which a code may be said to become obsolete and subject to a rather general revision is speculative. The chairman of the Merchants' Association Building Code Committee [10] of the City of New York stated that his staff found the building industry improving so rapidly that it was compelled to revise some of its first recommendations, replacing them by more up-to-date provisions. And this happened within the space of three years. The author of the present study found slight evidence of continuous revision in the form of insertions, additions, or deletions. In one or two instances recent codes had been developed in the loose-leaf form to facilitate change. Unless local administrative discretion is exercised to a marked extent, it may be concluded that an unreasonable number of cities are being served by obsolete codes.

Although the analysis presented here is wholly tentative, there is unmistakable evidence that there is much to be criticized in the administration of building laws in smaller communities. In later chapters detailed evaluations of the content of these laws will confirm this conclusion.

LEGAL STATUS OF BUILDING REGULATION

In this section codes are divided, for convenience, into three general classes according to their administrative agency: (*a*) the local code, (*b*) the state department of education code, and (*c*) all other state codes. All three classes derive their legal force from the constitutional provision which guarantees the general promotion of public health, public safety, and public morals. The three classes are not, however, accorded equally liberal interpretations

[10] *New York Times*, January 15, 1932.

of what constitutes public health, safety, and morals. The requirements and restraints of the local code have been limited to a jurisdiction over construction aspects that have a clear and immediate relationship to safety and health. Its authority resides in a delegated police power which, while safeguarding life and health, must not trespass on the sacred rights of use of property. Its prohibitive measures may not deprive an owner of the full or partial use of his property, unless there be unmistakable evidence that by so doing some definite menace to life or health has been averted.

Since frequent reference will be made in this study to the constitutional limitations of the police power and the consequent effects upon local school building regulations, it is essential to clarify the issue to some extent. The nature of the police power as it applies to the whole range of its jurisdiction has been defined by Freund in a rather general way.

> From the mass of decisions in which the nature of the power has been discussed, and its application either conceded or denied, it is possible to evolve at least two main attributes or characteristics which differentiate the police power: it aims directly to secure and promote the public welfare, and it does so by restraint and compulsion.[11]

In a further discussion Freund indicates that American constitutional law has studiously sought to prevent the police power from becoming an agency for the promotion of economy, convenience, or efficiency. The contention is that such powers lead readily to legislation which might be interpreted in favor of classes or groups in society. Thus, judicial opinion,[12] guided by precedent and statutory provision, frowns upon attempts to legislate into local building ordinances any measures which may have for their purpose the preservation of plant values, securing convenience, fitness of arrangement, or architectural appearance. The effects of these limitations are noticeable in the sections of the local building codes which deal directly or indirectly with schools. Legally these sections cannot prescribe measures which will secure educational fitness or adaptability.

In contrast to this limitation upon the local codes, the state codes appear to have extended their area of jurisdiction to include provisions relating to certain plant characteristics which would

[11] Ernst Freund, *Police Power*, p. 4.

[12] "The Enforcement of Building Code Provisions," *The American City*, pp. 6–8, January 1923.

probably be held void in a municipal code. There is a rather close distinction between the authorities exercised by the state as it supervises education and protects the safety of its citizens. In the first part of the quotation below is seen the source of the powers which a state department of education exercises as it supervises the educational aspects of school construction; in the second part is seen the source of power as it prescribes safety requirements.

> The state places its corporate and proprietary resources at the disposal of the public by the establishment of improvements and services of different kinds; and it exercises its compulsory powers for the prevention and anticipation of wrong by narrowing common law rights through conventional restraints and positive regulations which are not confined to the prohibition of wrongful acts. It is this latter kind of state control which constitutes the essence of the police power. The maxim of this power is that every individual must submit to such restraints in the exercise of his liberty or of his rights of property as may be required to remove or reduce the danger of the abuse of these rights on the part of those who are unskilful, careless or unscrupulous.[13]

Thus, the tentative Rules and Regulations for School Building Construction issued by the Department of Public Instruction of Pennsylvania have been drafted under the same type of welfare clause that gives constitutional force to the municipal code, but its prescriptions cover a broader conception of public health and welfare. In accordance with this vested authority the state code incorporates standards of accessibility, environment, orientation, size of site, and other similar provisions.

> The State Council of Education shall have the power, and its duty shall be: (*f*) To prescribe rules and regulations for the sanitary equipment, and the inspection of school buildings, and to take such action as it may deem necessary and expedient to promote the physical and moral welfare of the children in the public schools of this Commonwealth.[14]

These standards, however, are not positive in their nature, and are couched in terms which permit a rather wide latitude in the exercise of administrative discretion. The best interests of one community might conceivably be served by the rigid application of these standards, while such application might work a distinct hardship on another community. The chief value of these state requirements lies in their flexibility, permitting adjustment to varying circumstances and avoiding an undesirable standardiza-

[13] Ernst Freund, *op. cit.*, p. 6.

[14] *Pennsylvania School Law*, Art. LXI, Sec. 6102 (f).

tion of restraints and compulsions. Although local codes exercise extensive control over school building construction, none of their provisions have been framed to cover these indeterminate requirements. Their field of jurisdiction has been confined until very recently to those requirements which are unvarying in their application.

But health and safety status are, generally speaking, by no means conspicuous for the use of discretionary powers; on the contrary, in much of that legislation such powers are conspicuously absent . . . many building codes are framed with a minimum of administrative discretion, practically all regulation being limited to requirements capable of standardization . . .[15]

In response to public demand, and as a result of general municipal expansion, there has been a general trend during the past quarter century toward investing police power of the local code with ever widening jurisdiction. In this period of enlightened city planning and zoning, the restrictions of the police power as noted in the quotation below seem rather antiquated.

The offensiveness must as a rule consist in actual physical discomfort, or in a violation of the sense of decency; mere undesirableness by reason of social or other prejudices is not sufficient, not even if it leads to a depreciation of property. Thus a cemetery cannot without aggravating circumstances be declared a nuisance.[16]

Since the time when Freund made his analysis, a profound change appears to have taken place. In 1917 Bassett reviewed again the scope of the police power and found judicial opinion granting broader powers to city planning.

Our courts have wisely refrained from fixing an absolute limit to the exercise of the police power. The scope of the police power may increase as the needs of the communities increase. . . . The decided cases show that there has been a constantly growing field within which the courts will justify the exercise of the police power, and that the federal courts will uphold legislatures and courts of each state so far as police powers are concerned, unless there is a gross or discriminatory abuse of private rights.[17]

Today the courts will uniformly sustain ordinances restricting industries and enterprise to zones, unless clearly arbitrary, unreasonable, and having no substantial relations to public health, safety, morals, or general welfare. The term "general welfare"

[15] Ernst Freund, *Administrative Power over Persons and Property*, p. 98.
[16] Ernst Freund, *Police Power*, p. 160.
[17] Edward M. Bassett, *Constitutional Limitations on City Planning Powers*, p. 3.

is elastic, and as the social, economic, and civic aspects of community living change, so have the courts permitted the meaning of general welfare to change. A generation ago a cemetery was held to be without the control of police power. Current judicial opinion holds that the operation of mortuaries, funeral homes, drug stores, garages, and the like, is subject to regulation by the police power of the city.[18] Apparently this power is extended to regulate conditions which exist, so as to bring out of them the greatest welfare of the people by promoting public convenience or general prosperity.

> Reasonable building ordinance may be enacted under police power to protect communities, health, safety, morals, or general welfare, and to regulate business.[19]

When the courts begin using the terms "convenience," "comfort," or "prosperity," in designating probable areas of jurisdiction of the police power, it is possible only to speculate as to future developments. This is illustrated by the changed attitude toward governmental control of building design and appearance. A generation ago compulsory measures to preserve aesthetic values would have been held void by the courts as an infringement on private rights.

> General municipal building regulations in this country are enacted exclusively in the interest of health or safety. . . . In America buildings have never been controlled by law with a view to securing beauty or symmetry, whereas such regulations are not unknown in Europe.[20]

Recently there have been a few tentative efforts to clothe the municipal authorities in this country with power to secure and preserve artistic values in buildings. Zoning regulations achieve this result indirectly, and the courts have already signified a partial approval. A recent municipal code frankly makes the architectural appearance of a building a factor in the denying or granting of a permit.

> While zoning ordinance cannot be sustained merely on aesthetic grounds, that may be considered in connection with the general welfare.[21]
>
> Every building or structure hereafter constructed, erected, or enlarged

[18] State *v.* City of Miami, *Southern Reporter*, Vol. 134, p. 541.
Commonwealth *v.* Dillon, *North Eastern Reporter*, Vol. 178, p. 521.
Shumaker *v.* Borough of Dalton, *Federal Reporter*, Vol. 51 (2d), p. 793.

[19] Del Fanta *v.* Sherman, *Pacific Reporter*, Vol. 290, p. 1087.

[20] Ernst Freund, *Police Power*, p. 164.

[21] Appeal of Kerr, *Pennsylvania State Reports*, Vol. 294, p. 246.

shall be so designed and constructed as to be suitable to its environment from an architectural standpoint.[22]

The attitude of the courts on any controversy arising from provisions like this will have a profound effect upon future attempts by communities to develop pleasing effects through the control of building design. There appears, however, to be invested in the state an uncontested authority to supervise the construction of schools and other public buildings with a view toward securing desirable architectural effects.

Thus, there is definite statutory provision for the supervision of the architectural appearance of school buildings in Pennsylvania, except in cities of the first and second class. This control is vested in a State Art Commission which examines and approves or disapproves the plans which are required by law to be submitted.

Two very significant facts apparent in the comparison between state and local school building regulations are that the former prescribe for the safe construction, educational fitness, and in many instances the economical planning of schools, while the latter are limited to considerations of safety. As was noted earlier in this chapter, there is centralized jurisdiction of various degrees over the safe construction of schools in a majority of the states. As may be inferred from this discussion, there is coming to be more and more duplication of function. Compliance must be made with the local code and the state codes alike. Submission of plans, revisions to comply with review, payment of fees, and the time and service consumed under dual control are costly beyond justification.

From the standpoint of efficiency, economy, and safety, it would appear desirable to lodge complete control in that instrument which is not hampered by the limitations of the police power, which may command the services of competent specialists in both the educational and technical phases of construction, and which has at its disposal the facilities for administration, revision, and research.

SOME HISTORICAL ASPECTS OF BUILDING REGULATION

Regulation of building construction has been a function of government from earliest times. The Code of Hammurabi,

[22] Municipal Code of the Village of Winnetka, Ill., *Building Code*, Art. 5, Sec. 443, 1932.

King of Babylon about 2250 B.C., includes the rudiments of construction requirements.

> If a builder build a house for a man and do not make its construction firm, and the house which he has built collapse and cause the death of the owner of the house, that builder shall be put to death.[23]

The early Roman Law, which became the basis for the development of law throughout the civilized world, provided for definite restrictions on building heights to protect the prospect and light of neighboring structures.[24] Later Augustus introduced a law which limited the height of buildings to seventy feet, on account of the frequent ruins which had occurred. After the burning of Rome, Nero restricted the height of buildings. Trajan limited the height of houses to sixty feet, giving as a reason the liability of failure and the ruinous expense of such an event taking place. According to the laws of the Twelve Tables of Rome, every habitation was required to be surrounded by an open space at least two and one-half feet wide. This reservation was for the purpose of facilitating repairs, for protection against fire, and to secure ventilation. Comprehensive building laws were enacted in London as early as the year 1189.[25] The proceedings of the Common Council of the City of New York record the appointment of building inspectors in 1676, but give no information as to the extent of their functions.

The legislature of the State of New York enacted building laws for the City of New York prior to the year 1815, and subsequent legislatures amended and expanded these laws until 1882 when the City promulgated its first code. Specific mention was made of school building construction in the laws of 1849, and in Chapter 356, Section 19, of the Laws of New York, 1862, there appears a provision for fireproofing of doors, blinds, or shutters on every window and entrance above the first story of a schoolhouse, where the same do not open on a street.

The mechanics of code drafting in later periods follow a pattern which seeks to simplify arrangement by classifying buildings under broad categories, and then setting up the requirements in terms of these categories rather than in terms of individual

[23] Robert Francis Harper, *The Code of Hammurabi*, pp. 81–82.

[24] Frank Burton, "History of Building and Fire Prevention Codes," *National Fire Protection Association Quarterly*, pp. 364–79.

[25] Fitz-Elwyne's Assiz of Buildings, I Richard I (1189), "The Pioneer Building Ordinance," *National Municipal Review Supplement*, Vol. 17, pp. 555–63, 1928.

types of buildings. Thus, the municipal code of today contains but brief reference to the schoolhouse, but its requirements for public buildings are exhaustive.

SUMMARY

The available evidence indicates that school building construction is governed throughout the country by state and local laws with varying degrees of wasteful duplication. A system, or lack of system, which employs a multiplicity of reviewing agencies on both the state and the local level must obviously occasion needless delays and expenditures.

School building operations in municipalities are subject to very exacting requirements whenever the state and the city have enacted comprehensive building laws. There are, however, approximately 250 cities in the United States with populations of over 5,000 which construct, maintain, and operate school buildings without the jurisdiction of a local building code and with only very insignificant supervision by the state.

State schoolhousing codes administered by departments of education, seek to promote safety, economy, and educational efficiency in construction. Their provisions range from the type which is highly standardized and unvarying in application to the type which is elastic, permitting a reasonable adaptation to individual situations. Local building codes, in contrast, are written with a minimum of flexibility. Their provisions are restricted to controls which can be standardized and which are unvarying in their application.

The police power, from which the local building code derives its authority, is, by constitutional law and judicial opinion, positively limited to measures of safety which are tangible, objective, and universal in application. All things affected by subjective valuations, such as the aesthetic appearance of buildings, are quite definitely outside the scope of the local building code.

It is within reason, and in harmony with the best interests of education, to propose that the state code, which possesses the necessary powers to regulate all phases of construction, be constituted the sole legal control over local school building operations.

CHAPTER II

THE CHARACTER OF THE SCHOOLHOUSE AND ITS STATUS IN CODE CLASSIFICATION OF BUILDINGS

CLASSIFICATION OF ALL TYPES OF BUILDINGS

THE development of municipal building regulations, involving the codification of numerous and fragmentary bits of legislation, has resulted in a standardized, compact, and inclusive building code. The multiplicity and variety of requirements, applying to a jurisdiction equally diversified and complicated, have caused building codes to assume a condensed form which, in the interests of brevity and economy in production, seeks to provide blanket requirements for related types of structures. The general method employed distributes buildings into major categories on the bases of occupancy and use. All conceivable types of buildings, ranging from billboards to skyscrapers, are assembled under a few appropriate head titles and subtitles. The predominating plan[1] distributes buildings into three main divisions: "Public Buildings," "Business Buildings," and "Residence Buildings." The school building, obviously, is classified as a public building, and is thus subject to all the compulsions and restraints established for public buildings except in codes where special provisions or waivers are indicated.

The plan used in the Denver code[2] is typical of the three-way major classification.

CLASSIFICATION

SEC. 26. CLASSIFICATION OF BUILDINGS BY OCCUPANCY—All buildings shall be classified according to their use or occupancy under one of the following groups:

(*a*) GROUP I. PUBLIC BUILDINGS—Public buildings shall be construed to include all buildings or structures accessible to the public and in which people may congregate for civil, political, educational, religious, amusement or transportation purposes, or in which they may voluntarily or forcibly be detained

[1] See Table 6, page 44. Eleven of the twenty-three codes employed this plan.

[2] City and County of Denver, *Building Ordinance*, Art. III, Sec. 26, p. 13, 1926.

or housed for safety, observation, or care. These occupancies shall be divided into the Classes A and B.

Class A.

Armories	Asylums
Banks	Detention Buildings
City Halls	Police Halls
Court Houses	Hospitals
Film Exchanges	Nurseries
Museums	Railway Passenger Stations
Theatres	

Class B.

Amusement Halls	Libraries
Churches	Lodge Rooms
Colleges	Public Halls
Exhibition Halls	Schools
Bath Houses	

(*b*) GROUP II. BUSINESS BUILDINGS—Business buildings shall be construed to mean and include all structures used for or adapted to the transaction of business, the operation of machinery, the manufacture or storage of machinery or materials, the housing of livestock or for any other industrial purpose. The occupancies shall be divided into Classes C and D.

Class C.

Factories	Stables
Lofts	Warehouses
Office Buildings	Workshops
Printing Houses	Department Stores
Restaurants	Stores
Mercantile Buildings	

Class D.

Car Barns	Ice Houses
Foundries	Dry Cleaning
Light and Power Plants	Railway Freight Stations

Special industry buildings, constructed and occupied exclusively for commercial purposes or industry and not otherwise classified, such as:

Coffee Roasters	Sugar Refineries	Rendering Plants
Cooperage Shops	Laboratories	Smoke Houses
Grain Elevators	Oil Houses	Refrigerator Plants
Malt Houses	Refineries	Slaughter Houses
Soap Factories	Public Garages	

(*c*) GROUP III. RESIDENCE BUILDINGS—Residence buildings shall be construed to mean and include all buildings in which sleeping accommodations or housekeeping units are provided, and shall be divided into separate classes to provide the various requirements.

Class E. Apartments, clubhouses and studios, with more than two housekeeping units or ten sleeping rooms; dormitories, hotels, and lodgings. A basement designed for occupancy for more than the family of either a janitor or a caretaker, shall be deemed a story for the purpose of this class.

Class F. Dwellings and all other residence buildings not specified in Class E.[3]

[3] City and County of Denver, *Building Ordinance*, Art. III, Sec. 26, p. 13, 1926.

The objective sought in this classification is to eliminate, as far as possible, the expense involved in developing and administering separate codes for a score or more of buildings. Insofar as effecting economies in drafting, publishing, and administering the code is concerned, the objective has been achieved. How nearly these economies would balance the added costs imposed by excessive and general requirements in the actual erection of buildings can scarcely be estimated. It is extremely doubtful if these economies can be justified when reduced building efficiency and increased hazard to life and health are direct results of the attempt to fit general requirements to widely varying situations. A school building under process of construction at the time of writing illustrates this point. The local code prescribed general requirements in such a manner that confusion arose as to their application to the school building. In order to satisfy the regulations, certain alterations estimated to cost $100,000 were prescribed. This is probably an extreme case, but it serves to indicate that costs in code production can be offset easily by the economies resulting from a greater differentiation of requirements for individual types of buildings. The estimated cost of altering only one building in the case cited exceeded the cost of drafting the entire Proposed Code for the City of New York.

The three-way scheme of classification assumes that public buildings, business buildings, and residence buildings present three distinct types of hazard. Whether this procedure adequately differentiates the three classes on the basis of actual hazards to life and property can be determined only by a searching analysis of all the factors involved in hazard. It is commonly agreed that the degree of hazard encountered in any building is dependent upon five major elements: (1) the extent of human utilization, (2) the character and status of occupants, (3) the contemplated activities of the occupants, (4) the physical contents of the building, and (5) the location of the building with respect to neighboring hazards.

Consider the extent of the human utilization factor. Its influence on hazard determines minimum requirements for stairways, exits, ventilation, toilet facilities, live floor loads, and similar building features. But certain public buildings—the bathhouse, jail, and hospital, for instance—do not house the same number of occupants per unit of floor area as do the church and the school. In this respect, bathhouses, hospitals, and jails more nearly resemble buildings in other categories, such as residences and office buildings. Were the extent of human utilization the only factor, the classification would break down entirely with new alignments under different categories taking its place.

The status and character of the occupants are less definite factors in hazard. Physical conditions, as health and stature, however, are valid and important considerations. The status of occupants who are under legal compulsion to enter and remain within the buildings has a peculiar significance as opposed to the status of persons who voluntarily enter buildings and assume risks. Should a classification be attempted on the bases of these factors, there would be another and different distribution.

The contemplated activity of the occupants is probably the most diversified of the five factors. If a classification on this basis were carried to a final and logical conclusion, there would be almost as many separate categories as there are building types. Practical application must limit the classification to a reasonable number of divisions. The manner and extent to which this classification would disturb the traditional alignment could be revealed only after an exhaustive study of the activities. It is clear, however, even from casual observation that more extensive diversities exist among certain buildings within the same class than exist among certain buildings of different classes. Thus, the educational activities of pupils more nearly resemble the activities of patrons of clubhouses and studios in the residence class than they do the activities of patients or attendants of a hospital in the school's own class.

The combustible nature of the physical contents of a building constitutes one of the most definite and measurable influences on hazard to life and property. Nevertheless, the usual classification fails, in certain instances, to recognize this factor. This is well illustrated in the classification schedule on pages 19–20 where schools, film exchanges, and bathhouses are associated in one class. The difference in the combustibility of contents and sources of fire ignition in these three types of buildings is too obvious to need further elaboration.

The exposure of a building to other structures or conditions of a hazardous nature is also considered in the determination of requirements. Thus, in congested city areas these requirements assume importance in two ways: first, in securing adequate exterior protection against hazards from without; and, second, in securing interior protections to reduce the menace from within. It will be readily seen, therefore, that isolation is a significant factor in determining minimum safety requirements. Of all buildings public or private, the school, except in a few metropolitan centers, is usually the most protected with respect to remoteness from outside fire dangers.

Building ordinances usually attempt to base requirements, as far as available data permit, on the five major factors discussed in the preceding paragraphs. It is significant to note, however, the large number of exceptions and modifications that must be made if these factors are to receive adequate consideration under the traditional classification. It seems, therefore, entirely logical and practicable to establish these fundamental factors as the primary categories, replacing the customary and cumbersome use classification. When this is done it will be possible, on the bases of experimental evidence and comprehensive survey, to assemble all structures of similar or somewhat similar human utilization characteristics into one group. For this group, then, standards for those structural features which are directly associated with the extent of human utilization (for example, exits and stairways) can be established with more regard for the individual needs of the group. Adequate consideration of the other major factors in their new rôles as primary categories may be reflected in uniformity and appropriateness of regulation. The natural result will be a simplified code with more economy, building efficiency, and security to life and property.

The analysis presented in the foregoing paragraphs is wholly tentative and is offered here only as a suggestion for further study. Nevertheless it is maintained that the process of reconstructing the classification scheme may well be attempted with such data and evidence as are available. The expense involved in financing research on obscure or debatable issues would doubtless be offset many times over by the accrued economies in subsequent building activity.

CLASSIFICATION OF THE SCHOOL AS A PUBLIC BUILDING

This investigation is concerned only with school buildings and methods of code classification insofar as these methods seem to affect the school. The procedures and factors developed in this section, however, may well apply to the entire range of structures within the jurisdiction of the building ordinance.

The assumption underlying the plan of including schools with other public buildings is that courthouses, jails, bathhouses, lodge rooms, and other similar structures possess an inherent relationship in occupancy and hazard that molds them into a composite building. A close analysis will fail to discover these fundamental relationships existing in a degree sufficient to warrant the establishment of inclusive building requirements so common to most codes. The incongruity of the alignment becomes more striking when the attempt is made to relate bathhouse and schoolhouse hazards. Certain unimportant and irrelevant characteristics are common to public buildings. It is absurd, however, to maintain that hazards are influenced by the mere fact of public attendance or that sources of danger emanate from public ownership and operation.

The school building, like all other buildings, is an entity with distinctive structural, use, occupancy, and administrative characteristics. Whenever significantly differentiating characteristics have been tangible, measurable, and well defined, the codes have generally made special provision for the school building. On the other hand, the influences on hazard of other less well-defined factors have been only roughly estimated or, in certain instances, ignored entirely in the determination of minimum requirements. In the absence of specific code prescription, administrative discretion frequently has taken cognizance of both definite and indefinite factors, and where the circumstances have seemed to warrant waivers of requirement, has allowed exemptions and modifications. The effects of the practice of establishing minimum standards and of granting waivers of standards on the basis of opinion or insufficient and inconclusive data have resulted in weakness of requirement where strength is needed, and severity of standard where flexibility might be much more desirable.

Certain characteristics which should form the bases for determining the needs of an individual class of buildings have been isolated in this section for further analysis because they seem to mark the departure of the school from the general class of public buildings.

CHARACTERISTICS WHICH DISTINGUISH SCHOOLS, OR ARE POPULARLY SUPPOSED TO DISTINGUISH SCHOOLS, FROM OTHER TYPES OF PUBLIC BUILDINGS

I. TRANSIENCY OF OCCUPANTS

The enrollment in a school has a comparatively low transiency rate. Teachers, other employees, and pupils, in their routine tenancy of the building become familar with its interior arrangements. If an emergency arises, the occupants of the school can proceed with minimum direction through doorways, corridors, passages, and exits. Transient or chance occupants of other public buildings such as hospitals, courthouses, and jails are not offered the same favorable opportunity to familiarize themselves with the various means of escape in the event of an emergency. Thus far the argument indicates that the requirements for schools might be somewhat more lenient than those for other public buildings. This reasoning, however, is predicated upon assumptions that have no sound bases in fact. The occupancy of the school, although more stable than that of other buildings is not entirely free from transiency. There are occasions (and they may be numerous) when the school accommodates visitors, recently transferred pupils, and congregations of adults. The presence or absence of these occupancies is a human variable that cannot be accurately determined as to numbers or frequencies. It is proposed, therefore, that provisions for building safety be calculated on the basis of the greatest need—the occasion when transients are present in the building.

2. ADMINISTRATIVE FACTORS

The occupants of a school building are under varying degrees of discipline and restraint. The pupils are practiced in certain desirable forms of behavior which facilitate orderly and expeditious group movement. Periodic fire drills in the schools are very definitely safety measures which are not practiced to any appreciable extent in other types of buildings. Administrative policies and practices with reference to smoking within the building, the use of matches and inflammables by children, the teaching of safety habits, and school housekeeping are factors which are popularly supposed to reduce the fire hazard in a school building. In buildings of other types, the adult is not so closely supervised, he is granted a wider range of liberties, and he is not usually drilled in certain specific modes of behavior in case of fire. These clearly observable facts indicate that, so far as the above factors are concerned, the school building rates a lower fire hazard than do any of the other public buildings. It cannot be argued logically from these premises, however, that the requirements and restraints set up in the code for other public buildings should be modified downward in the case of schoolhouses.

The fire drill has been defended in certain quarters as a reasonable basis for reducing somewhat the code requirements for schools. It is obvious, however, that the fire drill and the other practices mentioned in the preceding paragraph are administrative variables dependent upon human manipulation. The only justification for the substitution of a human variable for a constant and automatic building feature in securing maximum safety lies in positive evidence that the former will operate without fail in all emergencies. The same degree of reliability and constancy should be required of the fire drill and practices in housekeeping as is required of an emergency lighting or sprinkler system before the former can be considered as replacing the latter. In order to substitute for a required emergency side exit in a school auditorium, the fire drill must at all times empty the auditorium within the same time limits and with as little hazard as when the side exits are provided and used.

The information on school fires assembled by the National Fire Protection Association shows that fire drills have not met the ultimate test. While the data are not as reliable as might be desired, they are sufficient to establish the uncertainty of this administrative device. The failure of the fire drill, as shown by the number of disorderly exits recorded in Table 2, is conclusive evidence of its unreliable character.

It would be interesting in the case of fatal school fires to know just how much a factor a fire drill might have been in getting people out of the building, or how frequently lack of it was a direct cause of fatalities. The reports in this record, however, do not show these facts except in a few cases. The following tables do show, as far as data could be taken from the reports, how the exit was made in each case. Except in the case of dormitories no attempt has been made to separate day from night fires, as except in dormitories, the time would make no difference, the occupants being usually awake.[4]

[4] National Fire Protection Association, *School Fires*, pp. 53–54.

TABLE 2

How Exit Was Made [5]

Analysis of Methods and Conditions Attending Exit from Burning School Buildings

	Number of Fires					
	High School	Elementary School	Classroom Buildings	Shops and Laboratories	Miscellaneous	All Except Dormitories
Exit made in good order....	4	10	0	0	1	15
Some occupants killed or burned................	0	5	0	0	2	7
All got out—no data on how	1	3	3	0	1	8
Exit made in disorder......	1	3	1	0	0	5
Rescues effected with ladders	1	1	0	0	0	2
Not a factor *............	78	92	36	33	25	264
No data................	20	35	14	14	31	114
Total................	105	149	54	47	60	415

Dormitories

	Day Fires	Night Fires	Total Number Fires
Some occupants killed or burned.....	1	11	12
Exit made in good order...........	3	6	9
All got out—no data as to how......	0	8	8
Exit made in disorder..............	0	6	6
Not a factor *.....................	0	0	19
No data........................	0	0	55
Total........................	4	31	109

* By "Not a factor" is meant cases where the building was empty at the time of the fire, or that owing to the unimportance of the fire no attempt was made to empty the building, or that the loss of life resulted from direct burns, attempted salvage, etc., where the means of exit was not a factor.

Table 3, reproduced from the study by the National Fire Protection Association, refutes any claim that hazards, characterized as peculiarly under the control of the administration, are at a minimum sufficient to warrant any reduction in fire protection. Spontaneous combustion, a factor quite definitely under administrative control, ranked second in frequency as a cause of

[5] *Ibid.*, p. 54.

TABLE 3

CAUSES OF SCHOOL FIRES FROM NATIONAL FIRE PROTECTION ASSOCIATION RECORDS [6]

CAUSES OF FIRES	NUMBER OF FIRES IN EACH KIND OF BUILDING						TOTAL
	High School	Elementary School	Classroom Buildings	Dormitories	Shops and Laboratories	Miscellaneous	
Electrical causes	31	21	15	26	4	7	104
Spontaneous ignition	21	17	11	6	15	6	76
Smoking matches	9	15	7	29	1	10	71
Defective or overheated heating equipment	16	31	4	9	0	1	61
Defective or overheated flue or chimney	6	21	7	12	3	7	56
Incendiary	11	25	4	3	1	2	46
Sparks on wooden shingle roofs	5	21	3	5	0	2	36
Rubbish and litter	4	3	3	1	0	1	12
Lightning	1	2	6	1	1	0	11
Acetylene or gasoline torch	1	4	2	2	1	1	11
Ignition of flammable liquids	2	0	1	0	7	0	10
Sparks from stove or fireplace	0	3	1	3	0	2	9
Motion picture film ignited	1	4	2	0	0	0	7
Defective oil burners	0	2	1	1	0	3	7
Exposure	0	5	0	0	0	1	6
Ignition of chemicals							
Ignition of plastic floor solvent	2	0	1	0	0	1	4
Woodwork ignited by steam pipes	1	1	0	0	0	1	3
Miscellaneous known causes*	4	11	1	14	5	4	39
Unknown causes	62	96	36	55	13	38	300
TOTAL	177	282	105	167	51	87	869

* The original table supplied miscellaneous known causes in detail. They are omitted here as not being pertinent to the issue.

school fires; smoking and matches, incendiary, rubbish and litter were all important causes of school fires.

These tables of fire causes indicate that schools are not particularly different from other occupancies, as the more common fire hazards head the list. Seven items are responsible for 450 out of 575, or approximately 78%, of the fires listed in the N. F. P. A. fire record for which the cause is known.[7]

A typical instance of the failure of the fire drill is related by the National Board of Fire Underwriters.

Lest faith in the efficacy of fire drills alone be too implicit it were well to remember that at Peabody, Mass., about a decade ago, 21 children perished in a parochial school fire, although a successful "fire drill" had been conducted on the preceding day.[8]

[6] National Fire Protection Association, *School Fires*, p. 40.

[7] *Ibid.*, p. 40.

[8] National Board of Fire Underwriters, "Consider the School-House," *Safeguarding America Against Fire*, Vol. 8, No. 2, p. 1, February 1925.

Two principles emerge from the discussion and the evidence adduced in the above paragraphs:

1. No community can afford to jeopardize the life or health of a single child by relying upon safety measures which may vary in effectiveness with the practices and policies of changing school administrations.
2. When the efficiency and reliability of a safety measure are subject to the variations inherent in human manipulation, the operation of that measure in any emergency cannot be assigned a higher safety value than that exhibited in the instance of its weakest performance.

3. DISTRIBUTION OF OCCUPANTS THROUGHOUT THE BUILDING

It has been maintained that fires in school buildings, started during the hours of occupancy, rarely gain much headway before detection. The plausible reason for this is that the occupants are distributed in all sections of the building in such a manner that incipient fires are discovered and extinguished before they are beyond the control of the occupants. The elements of chance and human intervention enter again as indeterminate and unreliable variables. Table 4 shows that, although the greatest number of school fires start when the building is empty, the proportion of school fires occurring during the hours of occupancy denies any possibility of considering distribution as a substitute for building regulations.

TABLE 4

OCCUPANCY AT TIME OF FIRE [9]

Conditions of Occupancy of School Buildings at Time of Fire

	HIGH SCHOOLS	ELEMENTARY SCHOOLS	CLASSROOM BUILDINGS	SHOPS AND LABORATORIES	MISCELLANEOUS	ALL EXCEPT DORMITORIES
Empty at time of fire	75	86	31	18	18	228
Occupied at time of fire	13	32	11	10	16	82
No data as to whether occupied or not	17	31	12	19	26	105
TOTAL	105	149	54	47	60	415

[9] National Fire Protection Association, *School Fires*, p. 53.

4. HOURS OF OCCUPANCY

When buildings or portions of buildings have been planned to include sleeping quarters, ordinances have, under certain conditions, specified additional fire protection. The schoolhouse, naturally, would be exempt from such additional requirements if the criterion of sleeping quarters were applied. The business of sleeping, however, is only one manifestation of that general state of unpreparedness which has been the reason for more protection. With this in mind, consider more closely the varied activities of the children within the school. There are rest periods when the children in the kindergarten and in special classes actually sleep. Gymnasium activities, demanding change of dress and bathing, place the individual in a state of unpreparedness which approximates that during sleep. Were the whole educational program subjected to a searching scrutiny, there doubtless would be discovered other activities which contribute in like manner and measure to the unpreparedness of the school child. The conclusion is that the school child requires just as much protection as is required by occupancies which are permanently quartered in other buildings.

5. DEGREE OF HUMAN UTILIZATION

The number of individuals to be accommodated at maximum building capacity is the major factor in calculating requirements for means of egress, live floor loads, and similar structural features. Buildings vary significantly in the matter of these capacities, and no single formula will satisfy the group needs. Codes, therefore, have attempted to solve this problem by specifying a more or less arbitrary number of square feet of floor area per person for each type of building. Schools are generally assigned a ratio of one pupil to 14 to 26 square feet of floor area. The auditorium ratio is variously fixed at 5 to 7 square feet per individual. This differentiation is commendable as far as it goes, but it fails to weight properly the pupil stations found in the special rooms of the modern school. When accurate calculations are made on the true basis of optimum sizes of pupil stations in classrooms, laboratories, special rooms, and gymnasiums, the average pupil station for a total building may be considerably different from those specified.

6. COMPULSORY ATTENDANCE

Under compulsory attendance, codes recognize only two different types of public buildings—detention buildings such as jails and reformatories, and buildings which house voluntary occupancies. The school actually occupies a position midway between the two. Children are not forcibly detained in schools by the use of locks and other barriers; neither are they permitted to make a choice in the matter of attending school. In a sense the school is a quasi-detention building.

Schools, then, must be populated, willy nilly. A tenant living in a fire trap apartment moves out if he values his life. Similarly, if the local theatre is inadequately served by exits, one is not obliged to frequent it; nor is it necessary to register at an unsafe hotel, attend a church that is poorly built, or patronize a hazardous hospital. Generally speaking, a person may discriminate in choosing the roofs that shall afford him shelter, day and night, in sickness and in health.

With schools, though, it is otherwise. Parents of but modestly endowed children perforce must send them to a particular institution, as fixed by local ordinances. There, be the building good or bad, safe or dangerous—and in thousands of cases, literally, conditions are appalling from the standpoint of fire—these representatives of a younger generation remain for several hours daily throughout a school year, approximating two hundred days. And this younger generation, it should be remembered, comprises one-fifth of the total population of the United States, a vital portion which the country can ill afford to jeopardize since it contains within itself the nation's whole trust for the future.[10]

There is a current theory that because children are under legal compulsion to enter and remain within school buildings there exists a greater legal and moral obligation to safeguard their lives and health. The school corporation acts *in loco parentis*, and the authorities and responsibilities of the parent are thereby transferred to the school. A critical evaluation of the home-child-school relationships indicates that the school may reasonably be expected to supply those protections and safeguards which the home supplies, or which the home would supply if it could.

A thoughtful consideration of this characteristic should leave no doubt as to its bearing upon fire protection requirements for the school. It is proposed, therefore, that code-drafting bodies seriously consider this factor and give it due weight in the determination of minimum requirements for schools.

[10] National Board of Fire Underwriters, *op. cit.*, p. 1.

7. PHYSICAL CONTENTS OF THE BUILDING

The quantities and varying degrees of combustibility of the contents of buildings have claimed priority as factors in establishing minimum requirements in fire protection. The form of inquiry that has contributed to a more accurate measure of this factor is illustrated by the experiments of the United States Bureau of Standards.

A few years ago resort to estimation would have been necessary in any system of requirements based upon the severity of fire to be expected from various occupancies. Today carefully conducted tests, such as those performed at the Bureau of Standards under the direction of S. H. Ingberg, have provided valuable basic information. Present indications based on complete burn outs of typical office and record room occupancies, in test structures, with no attempt to limit the duration by water or otherwise, are that the maximum fire effects will vary with the weight of combustible contents as follows:

COMBUSTIBLE CONTENTS (Weight of furniture, flooring, trim, etc.)	APPROXIMATE B. t. u. CONTENT	MAXIMUM FIRE HAZARD (Destructive effect equivalent to standard fire test)
Lbs./ft.²		*Hours*
10	80,000	1
15	120,000	1½
20	160,000	2
30	240,000	3
40	320,000	4½
50	380,000	6
60	432,000	7½

The combustible contents referred to in the table represent the total weight of all combustible furniture, flooring, trim, etc. The maximum fire hazard given represents the period during which an equivalent destructive effect would be produced by a fire regulated to correspond to the standard time-temperature curve given in the standard fire test.[11]

The above quotation is followed by a table giving in detail the results of an exhaustive investigation into the calorific values of a large number of materials.

An appraisal of the calorific values of the contents of the modern school would doubtless set it somewhat apart from other public buildings. When potential ignition sources are con-

[11] Building Code Committee, *Recommended Minimum Requirements for Fire Resistance in Buildings*, p. 23.

sidered in addition to the combustibility of contents, the differences become still more apparent. The radio and audio-visual installations, manual and household arts equipment, and the increasing variety of instructional materials in laboratories and special rooms, have caused the school of today to assume more the character of a commercial occupancy than that of a public building.

8. CHARACTER OF ACTIVITY

The process of learning, as contrasted with the activities of other building occupancies, involves the extensive use of certain senses, such as hearing and seeing. The ratio of window area to floor area, the color and finish of walls, ceilings, shades, and trim, the placement of windows and blackboards, and other similar items, may profoundly and permanently affect the immature organs of sight unless requirements are set up in terms of the specific needs of the child. Experimental evidence, such as that quoted below, indicates a real difference between the requirements of children and adults.

> In the first place, it is necessary to compare the reactions of children to different degrees of illumination with those of adults. We have not yet carried this and the succeeding phases of the experiment as far as they must ultimately be carried, but the curves shown in Figure 4 [not reproduced here] which are from six children of eight to twelve years of age, indicate that the illumination requirements of young children are radically different from those of older children and adults.[12]

It is probably premature, but certainly pertinent, to suggest here that acoustical treatment of certain building features is a child welfare measure that might well be made mandatory through the police power of the building ordinance. As codes are now written, their blanket requirements leave much to be desired in the case of the school. Their attention seems to be focused upon protection from fire, with a minimum consideration for hazards which influence other aspects of health, welfare, and comfort.

9. INTERNAL CONSTRUCTION

The subdivision of the school into various units, some of which are standardized as to dimensions, has a distinct relationship to exit and stairway requirements that differs materially from that of other public buildings.

[12] Frank N. Freeman, "Illumination Requirements of School Buildings," *National Education Association, Addresses and Proceedings*, p. 345, 1919.

The generous allotment of space to classrooms, laboratories, special activity rooms, corridors, and stairways is another important characteristic of the school's internal construction. In few other public or private buildings are these fire hazards so pronounced. Hospitals, office buildings, and similar structures are subdivided by fire-retarding partitions at comparatively frequent intervals.

> The reason for the terrific rapidity with which many fires spread, irrespective of occupancy, is that stairways and other vertical openings are not enclosed; this, of course, in addition to the combustible nature of the materials used, the contents and the existence of large, unbroken horizontal areas.[13]

The problem of locating stairways or exits so that the farthest point in any room does not exceed a specified maximum distance from the nearest stairway or exit offers complications when large assembly halls and laboratories are to be served. The blanket requirements covering this point operated satisfactorily when the school building consisted of a series of identical units. The satisfaction of the needs of the modern school will be found in an adaptation of requirements to its diversified internal arrangement.

10. SANITATION

Children are less inclined to appreciate the dangers arising from insanitary surroundings than are adults. They also offer less resistance to ills induced by unwholesome environment. In other public buildings the adult may exercise, from the experience of his years, certain personal precautions to overcome any building deficiencies. It is maintained that school children should be exposed to a maximum of wholesome influences in this respect during their growing and habit-forming years. Maintenance of certain desirable sanitary standards should, as far as practicable, be on an automatic basis, removed from the variations of human control.

11. FLEXIBILITY

The methods and content of the educational program are in a constant state of flux. Even the most conservative must admit that the progress of a decade may cause certain school building features to become quite inadequate or even obsolete. The school

[13] National Board of Fire Underwriters, *op. cit.*

building is the one public building which may be characterized as the pace maker in this respect. Courthouses, jails, hospitals, and railway passenger stations have become quite well standardized, and little change may be expected in their basic design. The school, however, demands a flexibility in requirement that will permit ready adjustment to progress.

12. STATURE OF OCCUPANTS

Building ordinances have given only partial recognition to this most obvious and important factor. In attempting to fit a blanket requirement to a public occupancy varying in physical size from the children in the nursery to adults in a courthouse, the inevitable result has been to nullify for both groups the beneficial effects of regulation.

Children of elementary and junior high school age make a special demand upon appropriate plant characteristics. Children of immature years cannot, without injury to themselves, tread the stairways required by ordinance for public buildings designed for an adult occupancy. Other building features, such as the heights of windows and of blackboards from the floor, widths of doorways, specifications for aisles and seats, cannot be ordered in identical units for children and adults.

13. AESTHETIC CONSIDERATIONS

The traditional school of a bygone day was conceived as a mere shell in which to house the educational program. Later conceptions have capitalized upon the potentialities of the school building as a direct and significant influence upon the education of the child.

> The ideals of every person are influenced by trees, lawns, and beautiful buildings. The school is the people's investment. It should, therefore, be made an example of home improvement. It can be so developed that it will aid in the development of the artistic and aesthetic.[14]
>
> I would have the school building first beautiful architecturally and placed in a charming landscape setting with ample garden spaces, for the reason that one of the functions of education is to teach the love of the aesthetic. I would have the building as near perfect in workmanship and in the choice of materials as possible, because the children of the public schools are the artists and artisans of the future, and the school buildings in which they work day after day

[14] *School Buildings, Equipment, and Grounds.* Bulletin No. 52, Department of Public Instruction, Lansing, Mich., 1922.

will be their standard, and it must be a high standard if our craftsmen are to be masters.[15]

Modern school buildings impart, through intimate association, certain enduring ideals, aspirations, and appreciations to the children. It is proposed, therefore, that every element of the structure should be so designed, planned, and decorated that it will contribute to the social and individual development of the child. Architectural fitness as well as utility is a desirable attribute of any building, but the art and beauty of the general class of public buildings serve mainly as satisfiers and stimulators of the predetermined wants of adults, while the aesthetic qualities of the school serve in a double capacity as both satisfiers and creators of desirable wants in the growing child.

No one with eyes to see, least of all no young person, can be in the presence of noble buildings without being affected by them. . . . No longer is magnificent architecture the mere expression of the vanity of kings and emperors. It speaks, if at all, with the voice of a whole people. It becomes a necessary means of lending dignity to democracy. It is less an extravagance than some of the parts of our city pattern which would instantly be recognized as practical. It is, indeed, practicability in the highest sense. It is not ornament or grandiosity, but fitness, truth, order, and simplicity. Even in actual dollars it may cost less than the ugliness and chaos with which large parts of almost every modern city are afflicted. But whatever its monetary cost, it will pay for itself in greater richness of living.[16]

Without minimizing the desirability of incorporating beauty, symmetry, and harmony in all classes of buildings, it is maintained that the school demands an extra margin of attention in this matter.

Unfortunately, many school buildings throughout the country do not reflect in their physical assemblies desirable standards of architectural treatment.

Anything less than a building well adapted to its educational purpose and one which makes a distinct contribution to community development and beauty should not leave satisfaction with those who plan.[17]

Utilitarian considerations come first and command the best that architects and engineers have to offer. This is as it should be, but

[15] W. R. McCornack, "School Buildings as They Are and As They Should Be," *National Education Association, Addresses and Proceedings*, p. 364, 1919.

[16] R. L. Duffus, *Mastering a Metropolis*, pp. 248–49.

[17] N. L. Engelhardt, "Modern Ideas for Modern Schools," *The Architectural Forum*, Vol. 55, pp. 637–43, December 1931.

the functions of building beautification need not therefore be neglected. The reason for this neglect lies in the failure to appraise properly the dignity and character of public education and, what is more pertinent to the present issue, the lack of artistic skill and imagination of local planning powers. These deficiencies can be overcome by a gradual elevation of public tastes and appreciations, with the possible aid of some form of governmental supervision. The former is a slow and uncertain process and its operation in the past has not always produced salutary results. Admitting, then, that a measure of centralized supervision would be desirable, consideration of such a proposal projects this discussion into the controversial issue of whether building beautification is within the legal jurisdiction of governmental control. This issue was clarified to some extent in Chapter I, with the conclusion that present trends, as reflected in recent court decisions and code provisions, indicate an unmistakable expansion of legal jurisdiction in this direction.

Building regulations may, by the nature of their specifications, exercise negative, neutral, or positive influences on the artistic appearances of school buildings. There can be no justification for requirements which tend to disfigure a structure, or to detract from its otherwise acceptable appearance. In the second instance, it is strictly within reason to expect at least a neutral influence. In making out a case for positive influence, this proposal does not imply a standardization of artistry in building elevation, design, color, decoration, or assembly, in the same sense that factors of safety are standardized. Such standardization would lead inevitably to monotony, stagnation, and the ultimate elimination of that pleasing variation which has begun to characterize American school architecture. The proposal suggests rather a quasi-permissive type of supervision and regulation which, through its superior knowledges and skills, could advise, direct, and stimulate local school building planning. The functions of this supervision should be extended to an effective disapproval of gross violations of building and community appearance.

The bedrock of consistent and continuous civic growth and development is beauty—a truly great city must necessarily be a beautiful city. The recognition of this fact is slowly evidencing itself in legislation regulating billboards and the height and character of building, in the appointment of Art Commissions, in much of the work of civic improvement societies and in the architecture of our buildings, even of those devoted to industry. Ugliness is always a handicap. Beauty is a controlling factor in efficient living.[18]

14. MUNICIPAL CONTROL OF SCHOOL BUILDING CONSTRUCTION

The planning and financing of school building programs in fiscally independent school systems are functions of the school board and its executive officers. The operation and control of the schools have been delegated to local school corporations by the state, and the relationship thus established removes the schools from the immediate control of municipal authorities. In this arrangement the chief city officer, his cabinet or council, and the various municipal bureaus have little authority over the affairs of education. The administration of building ordinances by a municipal bureau is an exception. No analysis has ever been made, to the writer's knowledge, of the evil or beneficial effects of having this technical phase of the educational business placed in the hands of municipal authorities. If the experience encountered in fiscally dependent districts where the construction of schools is made the responsibility of city boards can be accepted as an index of efficiency, the plan may be open to criticism. The analogy is somewhat distorted, however, since there is a significant difference between the educational requirements referred to in the quotation below and the type of requirements laid down in typical building ordinances.

> The needs for and features required in a school building are highly technical matters. They involve an understanding which is most completely possessed by persons trained in educational philosophy and practice. For example, take the seemingly simple but tremendously important matter of how large a classroom should be. The size, of necessity, depends upon the purpose to which the school authorities intend to put the room. Who knows this better than the school authorities and who can better than these same authorities see to it that the building really fits the educational program which the building is to house? Under the present plan of school building construction in Watertown, the educational plan must be adapted to fit the building.[19]

Nevertheless, both types of control are peculiarly sensitive to the intrigues of city politics. Current literature abounds with illustrations of possibilities of graft and corruption in connection with drafting and administering building ordinances. If beneficial results accrue from the transfer of educational planning powers

[18] Morris Llewellyn Cooke, *Our Cities Awake*, p. 335.

[19] *Report of the Survey of the Schools of Watertown, Massachusetts*, p. 35.

from municipal bureaus to school officials, it seems reasonable to expect equivalent results from a similar transfer of the more technical phases of planning included in the building code. Trends are already in this direction, as is evidenced by the increasing jurisdiction of the building bureaus in state departments of education.

> The economical phases of the building code's influence are not generally understood. The code, which imposes certain maximum limits for the use of building materials, can stimulate and increase the use of any building material, and it can, per contra, reduce the use of any material of construction. Selfish interest is quick to recognize the economical potentialities of the building code and seeks to profit thereby.
>
> It is readily understood that if the building code is so constituted that it gives greater privileges for the use of one material and imposes restrictions upon the use of another and competing material, an unnatural, unjust and dishonest condition obtains which subverts true competition and is detrimental to public welfare.[20]

Akin to the factor discussed above, but not quite identical, is the contrast between requirements for public and so-called private buildings. There has been no organized body of evidence built up to indicate that public buildings might suffer more through severity or superfluity of requirement than do private buildings. Private enterprise, however, safeguards its investment in a personal way that is usually denied public investment. Tax monies are all too often diverted from their legitimate uses. It would be a comparatively simple matter to scale requirements upward, or to interpret them for the benefit of special interests in the case of public works, but the private owner will investigate with care the restrictions and compulsions placed upon his project. All this suggests the need of a centralization of control in that agency which has been regularly constituted the state's educational representative, and which may be expected to supervise construction in the sole interests of education.

15. CAPITAL INVESTMENT IN SCHOOL BUILDINGS

The safeguarding of physical properties by insurance is predicted upon certain actuarial principles. Thus, increasing building values are accompanied by a corresponding increase in monetary risks, with the required insurance protections becoming, by the same token, more efficient and costly. The concrete applica-

[20] See *The Building Code, A Symposium.*

tion of this principle is seen in the relationship between fire insurance premiums and property values on the one hand, and insurance rates and fire hazards on the other.

Municipal building ordinances are, in a very real sense, a form of cooperative property insurance, and as such yield to the principle enunciated above. The public, then, is entitled to an efficiency in building ordinance protection which is commensurate with the values to be protected thereby. The evaluation of a building ordinance on the basis of the total values it protects is beyond the scope of this study. The best that can be attempted is to isolate the values represented by the various building classifications, and, by so doing, tentatively assign to each group its relative protection needs. Exact appraisals of existing building values were not available for each of the classifications, but the data in Chart I can be considered reliable indexes of these values. As a matter of fact, the actual construction contracts, while not showing cumulative building values, are more accurate than appraisals.

Table 5 and Chart I were calculated from data supplied by the F. W. Dodge Corporation, Statistical Division, New York. The "All other public buildings" classification in the chart includes hospitals, institutions, city halls, jails, and military, naval, religious, memorial, social, and recreational buildings. This combination was effected so that educational buildings contracts could be compared with the total collective contracts of the public buildings group. It will be noted that the public investment in educational buildings is only a little less than the investment in all other public buildings. Table 5 shows the average per cent each group contract was of the total contracts on the original and more detailed classification base. Educational buildings represent more than double the capital investment of any other so-called public buildings group.

Due caution must be observed in drawing conclusions as to the fixed position of any single group of buildings on this scale of values. The rather sharp upward trend in public works and utilities and public buildings contracts during the years of an economic emergency is undoubtedly caused by artificial stimulation. This trend will, in all probability, fall in the opposite direction when normal building activities are once more resumed. It is significant to note the comparatively stable position of educa-

TABLE 5

CONTRACTS OF CLASSIFIED BUILDING GROUPS COMPARED *

Average Per Cent 1919–1932

Groups	Per Cent of Total Contracts
Residential buildings	35.6
Public works and utilities	22.5
Commercial buildings	13.8
Industrial buildings	10.4
Educational buildings	7.7
Social and recreational buildings	3.2
Hospitals and institutions	2.7
Religious and memorial buildings	2.0
Military, naval, and public buildings	2.0

* Source: F. W. Dodge Corporation, Statistical Division, New York.

CHART I

ESTIMATED TOTAL CONSTRUCTION CONTRACTS AWARDED IN U. S., 1919–1932 *

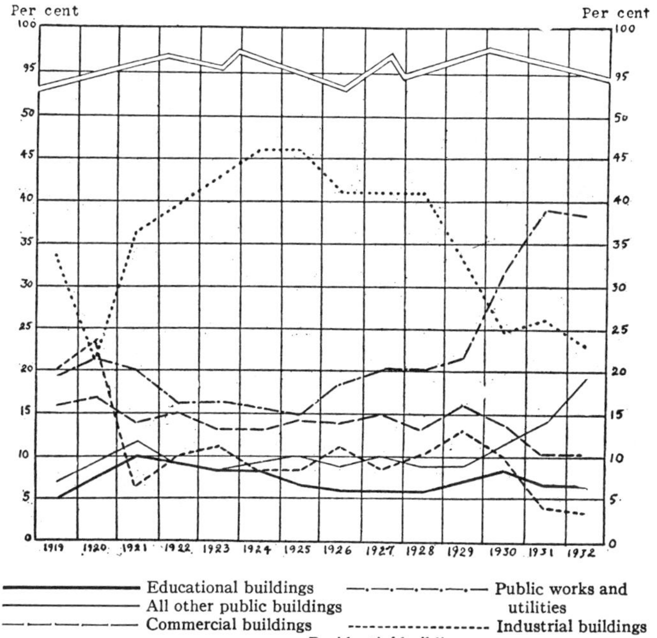

Educational buildings —.—.—.—.— Public works and utilities
All other public buildings
— — — — — Commercial buildings ------------------ Industrial buildings
.... Residential buildings

* Source: F. W. Dodge Corporation, Statistical Division, New York. Data exclude new construction and remodeling projects under $5,000. The data for 1932 are true reports for 37 Eastern states for the first seven months of 1932. Data for other years are based on true reports for 37 states with an estimate for the other 11 states.

tional buildings contracts over a period of years. Apparently, construction activities for this class are not so sensitive to fluctuations in public prosperity.

The importance of educational buildings, as measured by their position on the scale of values, has a definite implication for building regulation. While it may not be expedient to draft separate codes for school buildings, it may be an economy to formulate such ordinances with a better adaptation to the schools. When practical considerations compel the drafting of general requirements for certain groups of buildings, it is proposed that these requirements yield somewhat toward the needs of the group representing the greatest financial investment.

SUMMARY

Prevailing practices in the arrangment and form of municipal building codes seek to regulate building construction by establishing general and inclusive provisions for large classifications of structures. These classifications generally fail to secure the differentiation of requirement so essential to the needs of individual types of buildings. The advantages claimed for broad classifications are that economies are effected in preparing, printing, and administering the building code. It is doubtful, however, if these economies can be justified when increased costs and hazards and loss of building efficiency are the direct results of applying general regulations to buildings with widely varying needs and characteristics.

For purposes of regulation, the school building has usually been classified as a public building. The school, together with other public buildings, does not exhibit characteristics in use and occupancy which warrant the inclusive requirements so common to the majority of building ordinances. Under a closer scrutiny, building and use characteristics emerge which cause the school to make a definite and legitimate demand upon adaptation of requirements to special needs.

CHAPTER III

CODE REQUIREMENTS FOR FIRE RESISTANCE IN SCHOOL BUILDINGS

EXTENT OF INDIVIDUAL TREATMENT OF SCHOOL BUILDINGS IN TYPICAL CODES

THE purpose of Table 6 and the accompanying text is to pursue one step further the analysis of building code classification, and to show the actual methods employed in establishing blanket requirements for major classes of structures. The random selection of the codes was limited to twenty-six. Additions to the list would not have revealed any further significantly different practices. The structural features indicated in Table 6 represent only a fractional part of the whole range of building elements that could have been included. They are, however, major features and serve well the present purpose of illustrating common practices.

It is at once apparent that codes differ significantly in the emphasis they place upon the construction of school buildings. The Chicago Code devotes several pages to the school as an individual structure, while the codes in Tampa, Florida, and Fort Wayne, Indiana, scarcely go beyond the point of defining the school. Table 6 shows that certain structural features, such as live floor loads, tend to receive a maximum of individual attention in the codes while other features, such as stairways and bearing walls, are governed largely by general requirements. This difference in emphasis is due in part to the relative ease with which occupancy requirements can be isolated and studied, and in part to an assumed similarity of occupancy requirements. In the first instance the contrast is between live floor loads, a requirement quite readily determined, and stairways, a much more elusive element. In the second instance the illustration is found in natural lighting, a requirement which has been standardized for schools, but which has received little individual attention in municipal building ordinances. Although recent regulatory legislation reflects a disposi-

TABLE 6

CLASSIFICATION OF SCHOOL BUILDINGS AND EXTENT OF THEIR INDIVIDUAL TREATMENT IN MUNICIPAL BUILDING CODES

(Three Model Codes and Twenty-three City Codes)

BUILDING CODES	DATE OF CODE	NUMBER OF DIFFERENT BUILDING CLASSES		NUMBER OF TYPES OF BUILDINGS INCLUDED IN SAME CATEGORY AS SCHOOLS	SEPARATE ARTICLE FOR SCHOOLS	INDIVIDUAL PROVISIONS FOR SCHOOLS SPECIFIED IN THE GENERAL REQUIREMENTS FOR GROUPED CLASSES					
		Main	Sub.			Stair-ways	Stair-way Walls	Exits	Bearing Walls	Natural Lighting	Live Floor Loads
Organizations											
National Board of Fire Underwriters	1931	5		15		x		x			x
New England Building Officials Conference	1932	10	18	1	x	x	x	x		x	x
Pacific Coast Building Officials Conference	1930	10	23	12		x					x
Cities											
Baltimore, Md.	....	5		17							x
Cambridge, Mass.	1924	3	14	1							x
Chicago, Ill.	1928	9	15	1	x	x	x	x	x	x	x
Denver, Colo.	1926	3	6	9		x					x
Fort Wayne, Ind.	1926	14		1†							x
Fort Worth, Tex.	1928	3	14	1		x					x
Great Falls, Mont.	1917	6		‡	x	x		x			x
Hagerstown, Md.	1927	3	6	16							x
Houston, Tex.	1930	10		‡	x**						x
Kansas City, Kan.	1927	3	6	6	x	x	x	x		x	x
Los Angeles, Calif.*	1932			1	x	x	x	x		x	x
Louisville, Ky.	1926	3	6	13							x
Madison, Wis.*	1931			1	x	x	x	x		x	x
Manchester, N. H.*	1930										x
Milwaukee, Wis.*	1922										x
Minneapolis, Minn.	1922	7		1	x	x		x		x	x
New Orleans, La.	1927	3	6	21		x	x				x
New York, N. Y.	1926	3		21							x
Paterson, N. J.	1931	3		*							x
Philadelphia, Pa.	1930	7	13	8							x
Portland, Me.	1927	5	18	1	x	x		x		x	x
Providence, R. I.	1932	3	13	13							x
Tampa, Fla.	1926	3	6	16							x
TOTAL					9	13	6	9	1	7	26

x indicates provision. * No distinct classifications of buildings. † Separately classified but no individual requirements for the school. ‡ Described general class without naming any individual type of building. ** Brief and indefinite.

tion to recognize certain distinctive aspects of the school, the all-inclusive type of regulation remains the more prevalent.

The greatest variation exists in the manner in which codes prescribe both individual and general requirements for the school. In some instances the individual requirement will be exacting and detailed, in others it will consist of the slightest divergence from one of a series of general requirements. The latter is illustrated in the Model Code of the National Board of Fire Underwriters in which a brief, but in this case significant, modification for schools is inserted in an extensive series of general requirements for stairways.

(*a*) Treads and risers of required stairs shall be so proportioned that the product of the width of tread, exclusive of nosing, and the height of the riser, in inches, shall be not less than seventy nor more than seventy-five; but risers shall not exceed seven and three-quarters inches in height, and treads, exclusive of nosing, shall be not less than nine and one-half inches wide: provided that in schools the proportion and dimensions of the treads and risers may, in the discretion of the building official, be adjusted to suit the age of the pupils for which the school is intended. Treads and risers shall be of uniform width and height in any one flight.[1]

The exclusive treatment of the subject of stairways for schools, as illustrated by one of the several provisions for educational buildings in the Kansas City, Kansas, Code, is more rare.

Width of Stairways—Stairways in buildings used for the purpose of this class (schools) shall be equivalent in width to fifteen inches for every hundred seating capacity measured by the aggregate seating capacity of the auditorium, assembly rooms and school rooms; provided the number of persons allowed in such building at any one time shall be limited by the width of stairways available as exits.[2]

The most common form of regulating stairway construction provides a blanket coverage, with one of a series of paragraphs stipulating the class of buildings to which the whole section shall apply. Interpretation of the quoted paragraph below involves a thorough reading of all portions of the code relating to stairways, in order to determine whether the schools have been otherwise provided for.

(*n*) This section shall apply to all buildings and (not) otherwise provided for in this code, except "Private Dwellings," defined in this code.[3]

[1] National Board of Fire Underwriters, *Building Code*, Sec. 604, p. 60, 1931.
[2] Kansas City, Kan., *Building Code*, Sec. 1, p. 201, 1930.
[3] Fort Wayne, Ind., *Building Code*, Sec. 99, p. 36, 1927.

In this instance the section applied to the school. Another paragraph taken from the same code shows how confusion may arise as to the application of a section.

(*a*) Be it further ordained, That all public halls (not herein otherwise provided for), railroad depots, stores, warehouses, factories, workshops, club houses, and other buildings of like character hereafter built, in which, above the second floor, there is to be, or in which the provision is made for the employment or assembly of twenty to one hundred people, there shall be at least two stairways.[4]

Schools are not mentioned, but the reference to "other buildings of like character" (although it is difficult to see the similarity), and the fact that they are not otherwise provided for, interprets the requirement as applying to school buildings.

Codes are strangely silent on the subject of artificial lighting for schools. Natural lighting, however, is usually provided for in general requirements which follow somewhat the form adopted by the Model Code of the National Board of Fire Underwriters.

1. *Glass area.* The aggregate glass area of windows required by this article shall be not less than one-tenth of the floor area of the room served by them; provided that in habitable-rooms such glass area shall be not less than ten square feet, and in bath rooms it shall not be less than six square feet.

2. *Openings.* (*a*) In habitable-rooms and in bath rooms such windows shall be so constructed that when fully open the aggregate open space shall be not less than one-twentieth of the floor area of the room served by such windows.

(*b*) In other rooms the aggregate openable area of windows, doors, transoms and ventilating skylights that open on a street or on a court conforming to the requirements of this article shall be not less than one-twentieth of the aggregate floor area of the rooms served thereby.[5]

A careful reading of the article referred to in the quoted paragraph revealed no direct reference to the school building. The choice of interpretation lies between including the school under a very inadequate standard and excluding it entirely as not coming under the definition of the application. The latter seems to be the more logical construction. On the other hand, whenever the municipal code has reserved a considerable section for the schools exclusively there generally have been provided requirements for natural lighting based upon the peculiar needs of this occupancy. The paragraph taken from the Kansas City, Kansas, Code, the section on school buildings, is typical of this limited practice.

[4] Fort Wayne, Ind., *Building Code*, Sec. 101, p. 36, 1927.

[5] National Board of Fire Underwriters, *Building Code*, Sec. 502, pp. 47–48, 1931.

The total area of outside windows and skylights of each classroom, recitation room and study room shall be not less than one-fifth of the floor area of such room.[6]

The natural lighting requirements for schools are treated in greater detail in a later section of this study, but it is fitting to comment here on the marked difference in the adequacy of the general and the individual requirement. In achieving brevity, the code of the National Board of Fire Underwriters has failed to consider the highly important function of natural lighting for the school. The Kansas City Code, and a few more like it, have recognized these special demands of the school in their individual requirements.

If time and space permitted, it would be possible to add extensively to the quotations showing the manner in which the general requirements for groups of buildings must either ignore the school entirely or do more or less violence to its particular needs. The natural consequence of regulating school building construction under general requirements for related groups of structures will be revealed more fully as this study progresses into the analyses of detailed requirements.

CODE DESIGNATION OF CONSTRUCTION TYPES FOR SCHOOLS

Code classification of buildings according to occupancy and use is, necessarily, accompanied by a standardized classification according to types of construction. The latter may be defined as a classification based upon the fire-resistive qualities of various kinds of materials and their resultant combination in a finished building. Almost without exception the arrangement will consist of a series of types, beginning with the so-called absolutely fireproof structure,[7] and continuing through semi-fireproof, protected, ordinary, mill, and other intermediate types to the least fireproof, the frame building.[8] The usual method defines briefly the various types and follows with detailed requirements in separate sections or articles. Occupancies are then assigned to appropriate types of construction, depending upon the hazards involved, the

[6] Kansas City, Kan., *Building Code*, Sec. 1, p. 203, 1930.

[7] This study has preferred to use the term "fire-resistive" to designate that form of construction which provides the most efficient protection against fire. Since "fireproof" appears to be the more favored term in building codes, it will be used in the context which describes code practices.

[8] See page 53 for definition of the more common types of construction.

contemplated height of the building, the proposed protections, such as sprinklers, and the location of the structure with reference to fire districts.

At this point the first evidences of the effects of classifying schools with other groups of buildings are encountered. Construction classification in municipal building regulations, although lacking in uniformity throughout, follows verbatim or with minor variations certain basic patterns. Table 7 is a summary of the more common practices in classifying and establishing minimum heights for non-fireproof construction of schools. For the purpose of tabulation it was necessary to include under "non-fireproof construction" a rather large assortment of types, the more common of which were "ordinary" and "mill," sometimes called slow burning. This category, however, does not include frame construction. Codes quite generally prohibit the construction of all wood two-story schools. The sampling of cities shown in Table 7, limited by the availability of their effective codes, was made in such a manner as to furnish comparisons between the practices in cities of various sizes located in the different geographical areas of the United States. The conclusions below should be accepted, therefore, as indications rather than as final pronouncements on the total situation.

The most significant disclosure is the sanction of three-story non-fireproof construction in one-fifth of the total number of codes studied. In cities of more than 100,000 population, where requirements were made separately for schools, there was less variation in heights, with a distinct tendency to fix the limit for non-fireproof construction at two stories.

Ordinances in smaller municipalities differ markedly in their limitations on the heights of non-fireproof schools. The six codes that insist on fireproof construction for all heights, including one-story buildings, were taken from the smaller cities. On the other extreme, a larger number of the smaller city codes permit greater heights for non-fireproof construction than do the codes of the larger cities.

None of the cities with populations below 10,000 had building laws whose provisions could be interpreted as regulating the heights of school buildings. It is significant that a total of seventeen ordinances was so vague that the provisions could not be positively construed. All these were from the smaller city groups.

TABLE 7

NUMBER OF CODE CONSTRUCTION TYPES AND ALLOWABLE STORY HEIGHTS FOR NON-FIRE-RESISTIVE SCHOOL BUILDINGS AND THE EXTENT AND CHARACTER OF INDIVIDUAL AND BLANKET REQUIREMENTS

(One Hundred Cities of Different Sizes)

Distribution of Cities According to Population	Number of Cities	Number of Codes with Provision Lacking or Indefinite	Number of Codes with Individual Requirement	Number of Codes Specifying Indicated Number of Construction Types for All Classes of Buildings								Number of Codes Specifying the Indicated Allowable Heights in Stories for Non-Fireproof Construction of Schools						
				Not definite*	3	4	5	6	7	8	9	0	1	2	3	4	5	6
0– 10,000	3	3																
10,000– 50,000	34	9	9	3	3	11	2	3	3			5	3	7	9	1		
50,000–100,000	29	5	6	3	3	9	6		2	1		1	3	12	7			1
100,000–500,000	30		18	2		11	5	8	2	1	1		5	21	4			
Over 500,000	4		2			3		1						3		1		
TOTAL	100	17	35	8	6	34	13	12	7	2	1	6	11	43	20	2		1
Codes Prescribing Individual Requirement for Schools	35†			9%	3%	54%	14%	14%	6%				9%	77%	14%			
Codes Prescribing Blanket Requirement for Schools	48†			10%	10%	32%	17%	15%	10%	4%	2%	13%	17%	32%	32%	4%		2%

* No clear distinction between construction types.

† The 17 codes whose provisions were lacking or indefinite were omitted in the percentage tabulation. Thirty-five codes contained individual provisions for the schools, and 48 governed the school by means of blanket requirements.

Fewer than half of the codes specify individual requirements for heights of school buildings.

There is no significant variation among the practices of cities in the different geographical areas of the United States with reference to permissible heights of non-fireproof schools.

Although the analysis of the codes indicates a variety of practices in the number of defined types of construction, the prevailing practice established four major types. The construction of schools has generally been limited to four or five of the more common types.

It is evident that less attention, either individual or general, has been given the subject of school building regulation in the smaller cities than in the larger ones. The most efficient protections in the way of fire-fighting departments, water supply, and inspections are found in the larger cities where safety to life and property is emphasized by building ordinance. In the smaller cities where ordinances have a tendency to be vague, lenient, or nonexistent, these protections are usually of a less efficient character.

The lower section of Table 7 shows the effects of specific code requirements for school buildings as contrasted with the effects of regulating school building heights by general or blanket provisions. When provisions are drafted in terms of the peculiar needs of the school there is a distinct tendency for these provisions to be more uniform than the blanket requirement. This difference is especially noticeable in the columns indicating permissible heights for non-fireproof schools. Seventy-seven per cent of the individual requirements for schools limit the height of non-fire-resistive construction to two stories while only 32 per cent of the blanket requirements specify this height as the limit. It is also significant that blanket requirements prescribe limits ranging from an absolute prohibition to an allowable height of six stories for non-fireproof construction. In contrast, the individual requirements vary only slightly and show a decided agreement with current school building standards.

The specific manner in which heights of school buildings have been limited by ordinance furnishes evidence of the influence of both general and individual requirements. In the general requirement there has been a tendency to establish standards based upon an average demand of the group. Thus, in the Boulder, Colorado,

Code, schoolhouses are required to be of fireproof construction regardless of height.

> All school buildings, theatres, and hospitals erected in this city shall be constructed of fireproof materials, except doors, windows, floors, and interior finish, which may be of metal, wood, or other materials.[9]

This is, apparently, a rather stringent requirement. Interpreted literally, it prohibits the construction of one-story ordinary type schools. It is conceded that fireproof construction may be desirable for one-story heights in theatres and hospitals, but for the school, which shares in this requirement, the desirability is not so certain. Where special attention has been given to the school, ordinances have, as a rule, limited the height of non-fireproof schools to two stories. The quotation below is typical of the wording used in many of these provisions.

> Buildings of this class (includes schools) shall be of fire-proof construction, except that schools in which no pupils are accommodated above the second story, theatres accommodating less than 500 persons, and that part of a building containing an assembly room for less than 500 persons, may be of mill construction.[10]

An exception to this was found in the Great Falls, Montana, Code which specifically permits three-story non-fireproof construction of schools.

> Every building hereafter erected to be used as a school or convent building shall be of fireproof construction, if such building is more than three (3) stories in height.
>
> All other buildings must be of Class "C" Ordinary construction.[11]

In a few of the ordinances the limitations on heights have been conditioned by floor areas, building capacity, the presence or absence of large assembly halls, and the installation of automatic sprinkler systems.

> School buildings which are not over two (2) stories and basement in height and the seating capacity of which is less than three hundred (300) pupils may be built of ordinary masonry construction, unless otherwise prohibited by law; provided, however, that no such building shall contain an assembly hall above the first floor and no such assembly hall shall exceed in seating capacity the combined seating capacity of the classrooms by more than twenty-five (25) per cent, and, further provided, that the basement ceiling of all such

[9] Boulder, Colo., *Building Code*, Sec. 1, p. 9, 1922.

[10] Tacoma, Wash., *Building Code*, Sec. 22, p. 25, 1924.

[11] Great Falls, Mont., *Building Code*, Sec. 301, p. 179, 1917.

TABLE 3

NUMBER OF CODE CONSTRUCTION TYPES AND ALLOWABLE STORY HEIGHTS FOR NON-FIRE-RESISTIVE SCHOOL BUILDINGS AND THE EXTENT AND CHARACTER OF INDIVIDUAL AND BLANKET REQUIREMENTS

(One Hundred Cities in the Various Geographical Districts of the United States)

GEOGRAPHICAL DISTRIBUTION OF CITIES	NUMBER OF CITIES	NUMBER OF CODES WITH PROVISIONS LACKING OR INDEFINITE	NUMBER OF CODES WITH INDIVIDUAL REQUIREMENTS FOR THE SCHOOL	NUMBER OF CODES WITH THE INDICATED NUMBER OF CONSTRUCTION TYPES FOR ALL CLASSES OF BUILDINGS								NUMBER OF CODES SPECIFYING THE INDICATED ALLOWABLE HEIGHTS IN STORIES FOR NON-FIREPROOF CONSTRUCTION OF SCHOOLS						
				Not Definite*	3	4	5	6	7	8	9	0	1	2	3	4	5	6
New England States	13	3	2	1	4	2	1	1	1				1	4	4			1
Middle Atlantic States	7	2	2		2	2		1						4	1			
East North Central States	18	1	5	2		4	4	3	2	2		2	2	8	3	2		
West North Central States	11	1	3	2		5	1	2				1	1	5	3			
South Atlantic States	17	2	6	1		10	3	1				1	2	9	3			
East South Central States	7	1	3	1		3		1	1			1	1	3	1			
West South Central States	11	3	5	1		4	1		1		1		2	3	3			
Rocky Mountain States	7	4	2			2			1			1		1	1			
Pacific Coast States	9		7			2	3	3	1				2	6	1			
TOTAL	100	17	35	8	6	34	13	12	7	2	1	6	11	43	20	2		1

* No clear distinction between construction types.

buildings shall be plastered with metal lath and plaster and the heating plant and coal bunkers shall be enclosed in fireproof rooms.[12]

The analysis thus far reveals in a rough way current practices in governing the construction of schools with reference to allowable heights and types of construction. But the same type of construction does not afford the same degree of protection in all the codes. The variations in detailed specifications for the various construction types render the ordinary two-story school building a reasonably safe structure in some codes, while the lack of adequate specifications in other codes leaves the same height of ordinary construction little better than a fire trap. In the development of this point it is essential to consider first the more common types of construction and define briefly the characteristics of each. The four types most frequently used to designate different grades of fire resistance are given below as being typical of the provisions found in most ordinances. These types are basic and from them have been derived other intermediate types.

SEC. 59. CLASSIFICATION OF BUILDINGS BY CONSTRUCTION.—For the purpose of this ordinance, buildings shall be classified according to the method of construction as follows:

I. Fireproof Construction.
II. Non-Fireproof Construction.
III. Frame Construction.

I. *Fireproof Construction.*—A structure of masonry, protected steel or reinforced concrete construction.

II. *Non-Fireproof Construction.*—A structure having exterior masonry walls with floors and other interior construction wholly or in part of wood.

(a) *Ordinary Construction.*—A structure having masonry walls, with floors and partitions of wooden joist and stud construction. The supporting posts and girders may be of wood or of metal.

(b) *Mill Construction.*—(Sometimes called "Slow-Burning Construction.") A building having masonry walls and heavy timber interior construction.

III. *Frame Construction.*—A structure having the exterior walls or portions thereof of wood, or a building with wooden framework veneered with brick, stone, terra cotta or concrete, or covered with plaster, stucco or sheet metal.[13]

The definitions of ordinary and mill construction as quoted above reveal very little concerning those additional provisions so vital to the safeguarding of life and property in non-fireproof

[12] Sioux City, Iowa, *Building Code*, Sec. 243, p. 137, 1921.
[13] Louisville, Ky., *Building Code*, Sec. 59, pp. 39–40, 1926.

buildings. Further analysis is required to judge the adequacy of these types as they are set up in detail in various codes. For this purpose three major building features were isolated and their detailed requirements studied. Records of school fires indicate that these conflagrations most frequently originated in basements and heater rooms, and that losses of life and property have been most frequently occasioned by the spread of fires through stairways and hollow spaces in walls and floors. Proper protections in an ordinary or mill type school, then, would obviously consist of fire-resistive enclosures for stairways and boiler rooms, fire-resistive construction of stairs, and adequate fire-stopping in walls and floors. Provisions in the codes for fire-stopping and for protection to vertical openings were so complex and diverse that there was no practicable way of indicating the various practices without quoting verbatim whole sections from each code.

Requirements for stairway enclosures in the one hundred codes are shown in Table 9. Variety of practice almost defies any attempt to make tabular comparisons. The data as presented, however, indicate that most ordinances require some form of fire-resistive enclosure for stairways. Thirty-four ordinances permitted the use of combustible materials in enclosures, or were so vague in the treatment of this subject that no positive interpretation could be made. Only nine codes made individual requirements for school buildings, but in each case these ordinances were definite in prescribing incombustible stairway enclosures. Code-drafting bodies differ, however, in their concepts of what constitutes an adequate fire-resistive enclosure. On the one extreme, they have provided for the minimum, a one-hour fire separation,[14] and, on the other extreme, they have insisted upon the maximum, a four-hour absolute fire separation. In between the extremes are a number of different types of provisions, some of which are quite specific and others of which merely prescribe "masonry enclosure" or "incombustible partition," leaving the determination of materials and thicknesses to the discretion of the architect or builder. There was no significant difference between the ordinances in the larger and the smaller cities. It will be observed, however, that there is a tendency for the larger cities to give individual atten-

[14] The hour rating is based upon the length of time certain materials and combinations of materials will, without failure, resist the effects of fire. The ratings specified in the Tentative Specifications for Fire Tests of Building Construction and Materials, A.S.T.M., Designation C19–26, of the American Society for Testing Materials are the bases for many code requirements.

tion to the school and to frame their provisions in more definite terms.

TABLE 9

EXTENT AND CHARACTER OF INDIVIDUAL AND BLANKET CODE REQUIREMENTS FOR FIRE-RESISTANCE IN SCHOOL BUILDING STAIRWAY ENCLOSURES

(One Hundred Cities of Different Sizes)

Distribution of Cities According to Population	Number of Cities	Number of Codes with Individual Require-ments for Schools	Total Number of Codes In-definite or without Provision	Number of Codes Requiring Incom-bustible Con-struction *	Number of Codes Permitting Combustible Con-struction
0– 10,000. .	3	1		3	
10,000– 50,000. .	34		8	21	5
50,000–100,000. .	29		10	15	4
100,000–500,000. .	30	7	6	19	5
Over 500,000. .	4	1		4	
TOTAL.	100	9†	24	62	14

* Includes a wide variety of materials ranging from two to eight inches in thickness.

† The nine codes prescribing individual requirements for schools prohibit the use of combustible materials in partitions surrounding stairways.

The indefinite provision and the provision that permits the use of combustible materials in stairway enclosures are almost without exception found in those codes that specify ordinary, mill, or other types of non-fireproof construction without providing for additional protections for individual structures. In these codes the school with other kindred buildings is assigned to one of these non-fireproof types. Referring, then, to the detailed requirements of this type, it is found that provisions follow the traditional concept of this type: interior wood joist and steel construction for the ordinary type, heavy wood beam, plank, and steel for the mill or slow-burning type, and minor variations from these two for other types.

The analysis of provisions relating to the construction of the stair carriage[15] within the enclosure is shown in Table 10.

There is less agreement among the codes as to the required fire-resistive qualities of the stair carriage than of the walls or partitions enclosing the carriage. Approximately 75 per cent of the ordinances permit combustible carriage construction or are so

[15] "Stair carriage" is that construction which consists of the stairway landings and combinations of materials in the load-bearing part of stairs.

TABLE 10

EXTENT AND CHARACTER OF INDIVIDUAL AND BLANKET CODE REQUIREMENTS FOR FIRE-RESISTANCE IN SCHOOL BUILDING STAIRS

(One Hundred Cities of Different Sizes)

Distribution of Cities According to Population	Number of Cities	Number with Individual Requirements for Schools	Stair Carriage Construction*			Storage Space Under Stairs		
			Total Number of Codes Indefinite or Without Provision	Number of Codes Requiring Incombustible Construction	Number of Codes Permitting Combustible Construction	Number of Codes Specifically Prohibiting Construction	Number of Codes Prohibiting Storage but Indefinite as to the Construction	Number of Codes Permitting or not Mentioning Either Storage or Construction
0– 10,000..........	3	1		3				
10,000– 50,000..........	34	1	10	10	14	9	6	19
50,000–100,000..........	29		11	6	12	6	9	14
100,000–500,000..........	30	5	5	8	17	2	11	17
Over 500,000..........	4	3		1	3	1	1	2
TOTAL...............	100	10	26	28	46	18	27	52
Codes Prescribing Individual Requirements for Schools..............	10†		0	60%	40%	20%	20%	60%
Codes Prescribing Blanket Requirements for Schools	90†		29%	24%	47%	18%	28%	54%

* The bearing part of stairways as distinguished from enclosures.
† Ten codes made individual provisions, and ninety made blanket requirements for the school building.

worded that no positive interpretation could be made. Apparently, code-drafting bodies have felt satisfied that reasonable safety is secured by allowing non-fireproof construction in the stair carriage, provided that this construction is protected against exterior fire dangers by incombustible walls or partitions. The difference between individual and general requirements, as shown in the lower section of Table 10, is not so marked here, but there is an observable tendency for the individual requirement to specify a slightly higher degree of protection. This conclusion applies to the use of combustible materials in the stairs, but does not carry over into the provisions relating to the construction of storage spaces under stairways. In view of the fact that storage spaces under stairways present very potent fire hazards it seems strange that only 20 per cent of the individual and 18 per cent of the general requirements specifically prohibit the construction of such spaces. A paragraph taken from the Atlanta, Georgia, Code is typical of the manner in which many codes have regulated stairway construction.

> In fire-resistive buildings all stairs, platforms, landings, and stair hallways, including the flooring, shall be of fire-resistive construction. Storage of combustible material is prohibited within the stairway enclosure.[16]

The interpretation of this paragraph as allowing non-fire-resistive construction of stairs in non-fireproof buildings is confirmed by the detailed requirements for ordinary or mill type buildings. The provision regarding storage, since it follows closely the context concerning fire-resistive buildings, might readily be interpreted as applying to this type of construction only. The more reasonable interpretation, however, would recognize this provision as intended to prohibit storage of combustible matter within the stairway enclosure of all types of buildings. It should be noted that storage is prohibited, but no specific and literal prohibition is placed upon the construction of storage space. A total of twenty-seven ordinances treat this subject in the same way. In contrast to this type of provision is the requirement found in sixteen codes which positively prohibits the construction of storage space within the stairway enclosure. There can be no evasion or misinterpretation when requirements are drafted after the fashion of the following:

[16] Atlanta, Ga., *Building Code*, Sec. 45, p. 55, 1924.

In non-fireproof buildings no closet shall be constructed underneath the staircase of any story, but the space thereunder shall be left entirely open and kept free from incumbrances; but this shall not prohibit the enclosing, without openings, of the under portion of the first story staircases from the foot of the same to a point where the height from the floor line to the soffit of the staircase shall not exceed five feet.[17]

More than 50 per cent of the ordinances are silent on the subject of stairway storage spaces. In a few instances codes have contained provisions deliberately permitting the construction of storage space under stairs, provided the combustible portion of the stairs directly above is protected by metal lath and plaster.

Table 11 indicates a wide disagreement between codes as to regulations governing the construction of boiler room walls and doors.

TABLE 11

EXTENT AND CHARACTER OF INDIVIDUAL AND BLANKET CODE REQUIREMENTS FOR BOILERS AND FOR FIRE-RESISTANCE IN BOILER ROOM WALLS IN SCHOOL BUILDINGS

(One Hundred Cities of Different Sizes)

Distribution of Cities According to Population	Number of Cities	Type of Boiler		Walls of Room		Doors to Room		
		Number of Codes Requiring Low Pressure	Number of Codes with No Restrictions	Number of Codes Requiring Incombustible Construction*	Number of Codes Permitting Combustible Construction	Number of Codes Indefinite or without Provision	Number of Codes Requiring Fire Door†	Number of Codes Requiring Exterior Doors Only
0– 10,000......	3		3	1	2	3		
10,000– 50,000......	34		34	15	19	24	10	
50,000–100,000......	29	1	28	13	16	22	5	2
100,000–500,000......	30	2	28	24	6	15	12	3
Over 500,000......	4	1	3	4			4	
TOTAL............	100	4	96	57	43	64	31	5
Codes Prescribing Individual Requirements for Schools.........		15%	85%	100%	0	38%	54%	8%
Codes Prescribing Blanket Requirements for Schools............		2%	98%	50%	50%	68%	27%	5%

* Incombustible includes a wide variety of solid and hollow masonry construction of thicknesses ranging from four to twelve inches.

† Includes several different types of fire doors.

[17] Jackson, Miss., *Building Code*, Sec. 291, p. 112, 1930.

It is startling to note that almost one-half of the ordinances either permit combustible walls or are so indefinite on the subject that combustible materials may be used without positive violation of requirements. In many of the codes the only reference to boiler rooms was found in quotations like the following:

> Any woodwork, wooden lath and plaster partition or ceiling within four (4) feet of the sides or back or six (6) feet from the front of any heating boiler, furnace, bakery oven, coffee roaster, fire heated candy kettle, laundry stove or other similar appliance, shall be covered with metal to a height of at least four (4) feet above the floor. . . . In no case shall such combustible construction be permitted within two (2) feet of the sides or back of the heating appliance or five (5) feet in front of the same.[18]

To those who are familiar with the construction of the modern school, this type of requirement seems antiquated, far behind the dictates of good current practice. It seems almost inconceivable that this provision was drafted with the intent of including schools, but the breadth of its application and the absence of any other pertinent requirement leave no other choice of interpretation. The authors of the following regulation realized the desirability of adequate protection from boiler room hazards, but failed to put their convictions in the form of mandatory requirement.

> It is recommended that the rooms in which boilers and all other power and operating machinery are located be separated from other portions of the building by at least an eight (8) inch wall having a fire door at each opening and having no communication with the floor above.[19]

The lower portion of Table 11 indicates a rather decided tendency for individual requirements to specify minimum standards in harmony with best current practice. In contrast, the blanket requirements prescribe, either through omission or specific reference, non-standard practice quite as frequently as recognized standard practice.

For the purpose of summarizing the contrasts between the blanket and individual requirements for the building features analyzed in this section, the following six elements were isolated and stated in the form of standard practice:

1. Two-story non-fireproof schoolhouses.
2. Incombustible stairway enclosures.
3. Storage space prohibited within the stairway enclosures.

[18] Fort Smith, Ark., *Building Code*, Sec. 58, p. 31, 1923.
[19] Baton Rouge, La., *Building Code*, Sec. 180, p. 193, 1928.

4. Incombustible stair carriage construction.
5. Incombustible boiler room enclosures.
6. Incombustible doors to boiler rooms.

Indefinite or lacking requirements were accounted for as non-standard. There were six hundred separate items to be divided into two major categories: blanket and individual requirements. Each of these was then divided into standard and non-standard provisions. Table 12 shows that individual requirements for the school more nearly approach the standards set by current practice.

TABLE 12

EXTENT AND CHARACTER OF INDIVIDUAL AND BLANKET CODE REQUIREMENTS FOR FIRE-RESISTANCE IN SIX MAJOR STRUCTURAL FEATURES OF SCHOOL BUILDINGS

	INDIVIDUAL REQUIREMENTS		BLANKET REQUIREMENTS	
	Standard	Non-standard	Standard	Non-standard
Number	57	23	181	339
Per cent	71%	29%	35%	65%

EVALUATION OF CODE REQUIREMENTS AND CURRENT STANDARDS

In the preceding section certain commonly accepted school building standards were used to evaluate the adequacy of blanket code requirements as compared to the individual requirements for school buildings. It is the purpose of this section to submit evidence and argument that will definitely prove the inadequacy of those requirements which deviate from current standards in the direction of leniency. The validity of the assumptions underlying the development of current standards will also be questioned.

The standards below have been rather universally adopted throughout the country and are quoted here to initiate the criticism of code requirements and the analysis of the standards themselves:

1. Definitions:

For construction purposes, the American Institute of Architects has grouped buildings under five types as follows:

Type A—A building constructed entirely of fire-resistive materials, including its roof, windows, doors, floors, and finish.

Type B—A building of fire-resistive construction in its walls, floors, stairways, and ceilings, but with wood finish, wood or composition floor surface, and wood roof construction over fire-resistive ceiling.

Type C—A building with masonry walls, fire-resistive corridors and stairways, but with ordinary construction otherwise, i.e., combustible floors, partitions, roofs, and finish.

Type D—A building with masonry walls, but otherwise ordinary or joist construction and wood finish.

Type E—A frame building constructed with wood above foundation, with or without slate or other semi-fireproof material on roof.

2. Material:

Hardburned brick and steel or reinforced concrete are standard materials for construction of types A, B, and C. Terra cotta and stone are also acceptable.

3. Height:

No school building, except in very congested cities, should be approved which is planned for more than two stories above the ground floor. A basement should be used only for the heating plant, storage and similar service. Stories more than sixteen (16) feet high, measuring from floor to ceiling, should be rated as two stories. No school building of type D and E construction should be approved when it is planned for more than one story.[20]

The National Board of Fire Underwriters has approved substantially the same type of minimum standard.

In a general way it may be stated that schools of a single story need not be of fire-resistive construction in order to be safe, provided, of course, that there are individual room exits in the outer walls. Even two-story structures seldom require the use of fire-resistive materials throughout, if the floor areas are moderate and adequately protected exits are afforded. Schools of three stories or over in height, though, should be of the most improved fire-resistive construction, with divided horizontal areas and with stairways and all other vertical openings properly enclosed.[21]

The majority of municipal building ordinances which treat this subject also specify two stories as the limit in height for non-fire-resistive buildings with variations as to effectiveness of certain minor structural elements.

Standards, because of the very nature of the elements which they seek to control, have a tendency to become progressively obsolete with time unless they are systematically caused to yield to the demands of changing conditions. Rapid progress in the improvement of old and discovery of new building materials and the betterment of construction methods, the introduction of new hazards, and cost factors, raise the ever-continuing issue of re-

[20] G. D. Strayer and N. L. Engelhardt, *Standards for Elementary School Buildings*, pp. 10–11.

[21] National Board of Fire Underwriters, "Consider the Schoolhouse," *Safeguarding America Against Fire*, Vol. 8, No. 2, p. 1, February 1925.

placing outmoded standards by standards adapted to the present needs of public welfare and community economics. School building standards are peculiarly sensitive to these influences.

Certain well-defined considerations emerge in the re-appraisal of current code requirements and the popularly accepted standards for schoolhouses. Briefly stated they are as follows:

1. Adequate protection of life and health from fire hazards.
2. Adequate protection of property from destruction by fire.
3. Operation and maintenance of various types of construction.
4. Durability or longevity of various types of construction.
5. Capital outlay, insurance, depreciation, and salvage value of various types of construction.

A sixth influencing item might be included and identified as miscellaneous. It would incorporate the real and assumed characteristics of the school building as defined and discussed in Chapter II. These characteristics, however, cannot be considered separately from the five major factors, and will therefore be treated as contributing influences.

I. ADEQUATE PROTECTION OF LIFE AND HEALTH FROM FIRE HAZARDS

It is characteristic of progressive civilizations that humanitarian ideals and practices ascend to ever higher positions on the scale of social values. The care and solicitude that any society bestows upon its younger members, its aged, infirm, and unfortunate members, is a fairly good gauge of that society's advance in civilization. The palpable effects of changing attitudes toward these social virtues are seen in the increased sentiment in favor of child labor legislation, institutional provisions for the defective and helpless, correctional rather than disciplinary treatment of antisocial members, welfare movements of many types, and more recently in the gradual acceptance of group responsibility for the economic security of individuals. These changing sentiments and the material results of their application to social problems elude precise calculation. Nevertheless, their forces are real, and due thought must be accorded them in the approach to the issue of what in a modern democracy shall constitute adequate safeguards for the lives and health of the nation's greatest asset, the school children. It is proposed, therefore, that current standards in schoolhouse construction be subjected to a closer analysis to discover whether these standards have been significantly revised in recent years to keep pace with the newer ideals as expressed in the preceding discussion.

The two-story non-fire-resistive schoolhouse with protected stairways and corridors had its inception as a minimum standard approximately two decades ago. Between the years 1910 and 1920 there was considerable agitation for better and safer school buildings. The latter half of this period, especially, was marked by a pronounced public concern which found its expression in the published literature of the time and in the investigations and activities of the National Education Association. The records and proceedings of this latter body during the years 1917, 1918, and 1919 are evidence of this unprecedented interest. In 1917 the Committee on School Building Measurements of the American Institute of Architects issued its report which consisted, in part, of the standards quoted on pages 60–61. Thus, there came to be a rather general acceptance of the two-story partially fire-resistive schoolhouse as a reasonably safe structure. In the few instances where states had manifested an interest in the subject, it became a part of the state law; local building ordinances and the standards established by school building authorities incorporated it as a minimum requirement. It is not only interesting but highly significant to speculate on the forces that operated to bring about the acceptance of these higher standards.

> Since Collinwood we have sacrificed three hundred more lives in school fires, and the only reason why that butchery (sic) hasn't been higher is luck. With five school fires every day in this country, the potential is high; fortunately the vast majority of those fires have broken out at night or at times when the school happened to be empty. . . .
>
> Such luck can't last forever. And before it turns again it behooves us to set about remedying the conditions which invite disaster. That those conditions are universal was evidenced by a survey of several thousand schools in different parts of the country a few years ago which condemned 37 per cent of the buildings studied as rank fire traps. Whereupon the National Fire Protection Association, feeling that the proportion was much too optimistic, asserted that 90 per cent of our schools really belong in that dreaded classification.[22]

It is a notorious fact that a large percentage of the schools erected in the past were potential furnaces, shells of masonry with highly inflammable interiors. Fires were frequent and the ag-

[22] Alfred T. Fleming, *Is Your School a Fire Trap?* Reprinted with permission of *The Ladies' Home Journal* by the National Board of Fire Underwriters, New York, 1932.

gregate property loss throughout the country was staggering. It was the loss of life in major school fires, however, that focused public attention upon the menace of the non-fire-resistive school. The tragedy of the Collinwood, Ohio, school fire brought about more rigid state and local laws. In 1915 twenty-two children lost their lives in a school fire in Peabody, Massachusetts, and public reaction came in the form of an insistent demand for safer schools. The warning was sounded in all parts of the country in challenging statements. Civic and governmental bodies took up the cry, and an advance was made along the whole line toward better and safer schools. It is a sad commentary, however, upon the foresight of the educational profession and its allies in school construction, the architects, engineers, and builders, that human life had to be sacrificed upon the altar of progress. It is as though these responsible groups had acquiesced in the grim experiments which had been performed to determine the limits beyond which certain combustible construction should not be used.

Lack of foresight is not the only obstruction. There is the almost pathetic faith of the American people in cures rather than in preventives. They prefer to carry on until some disastrous consequence befalls them. Mandatory regulations to prevent the occurrence of disaster are secondary in importance to the provision to alleviate or control results. Our American cities are said to have the most efficient and best equipped fire-fighting departments in the world. Their primary function is to control results, to fight fire after it has started. In contrast to this, our laws, ordinances, and practices, designed to prevent the start of fires, are far less effective than those of the European countries. This attitude is reflected in the laws relating to the construction of schoolhouses. Numerous facilities are provided, many of them mandatory, to minimize the hazards after a fire has started. Chemical extinguishers, standpipes, fire alarm systems, fire detecting apparatus, automatic sprinklers, and outside fire escapes are typical of these provisions. All are important, but their inclusion should not be the justification for the omission of desirable preventive measures. In a survey of state schoolhousing regulations[23] in 1915 it was found that only six states had any provisions relating to fire-resistive construction of schools, while

[23] Frank Irving Cooper, "Standardization of Schoolhouse Planning and Construction," *National Education Association, Addresses and Proceedings*, p. 570, 1918.

nineteen required fire escapes. An extension of this survey[24] in 1920 showed that fourteen states had some form of requirement on fire-resistive construction and thirty-three had provisions relating to fire escapes. A similar survey[25] in 1929 indicated that trends continued in approximately the same way. The only defense, if such it be, for these practices lies in the economic pressure which may force communities to adopt fire escapes in preference to incombustible interior construction.

The discussion thus far has taken note of the approximate period and the apparent reasons for the adoption of present school building standards. Fifteen or twenty years have elapsed since the two-story non-fire-resistive school with protected stairways and corridors became established as a standard. The intention here is not to compare the occupancy hazard of the school of fifteen years ago with the school of today, nor is it the purpose to compare the economic factors of the two periods. The thought is limited to a comparison of the social ideals and attitudes of the two periods. As was pointed out in an earlier paragraph, notable progress has been made during the intervening years in many aspects of social relationships and responsibilities. The comfort, safety, health, convenience, and even prosperity of individuals have become more and more matters of group concern. But in this one small phase of the social structure, safeguarding the lives of school children from fire hazards, there has been no similar progress. What was good enough fifteen years ago is good enough today.

It is recommended here that steps be taken by code-drafting bodies and other influential and responsible groups to critically evaluate public sentiment to determine wherein its satisfactions, as measured by human values of today, may lie. It would not be surprising if it were found that the social conscience is in advance of written standards.

The fire protection prescribed by municipal ordinances for schools and other structures is presumably the expression of the popular will insofar as the drafters of these ordinances were able to interpret this will. The people in turn must have all the facts interpreted to them before they can make any intelligent choice.

[24] Frank W. Hart, *A Standard State Schoolhousing Code*, p. 9.

[25] H. M. McGowan, "An Analysis of State School-Building Codes," *Educational Research Bulletin*, Vol. X, No. 17, p. 461, November 1931. College of Education, The Ohio State University.

TABLE

ANALYSIS OF

(*Structural Features Contributing to Panic and*

School	Date	Number of Deaths	Origin and Cause
Lakewood School, Collinwood, Ohio	1908	175	Steam main on wooden joist Basement closet under stairway
St. John's Parochial, Peabody, Mass.	1915	21	Barrels of rubbish in basement Basement closet under stairway
St. Boniface College, Manitoba	1922	10	Smoking in toilet in one of the upper floors.
Cleveland School, Camden, S. C.	1923	77	Oil lamp on improvised platform in auditorium
Hope Development School, Playa del Rey, Calif.	1924	24	Probably incendiary—origin unknown
Rural School, Babbs Switch, Okla.	1924	36	Christmas tree candle and overturned lamp in front room
Beauval Mission School, Saskatchewan	1927	20	Furnace or chimney in the basement
Deering High School, Portland, Maine	1921	1	Engineer's closet containing clothing and personal belongings
English High School, Lynn, Mass.	1924	1	Paper baling room in the basement
Hochelaga School, Montreal	1907	10	Wooden waste paper chute
Negro School, Ashville, N. C.	1917	7	Boiler room—cause unknown
High Point School, Covington, Ga.	1922	2	First floor—cause unknown
Pleasant Valley School, Tyron, Okla.	1930	3	Pouring kerosene on fire

* Adapted from descriptive reports of the National Fire Protection

It is safe to assume that the patrons of the Collinwood, Ohio, the Peabody, Massachusetts, and the Camden, South Carolina, schools would not for long have countenanced the laws which permitted and invited those fearful fires had they been fully apprised of the conditions beforehand.

13

MAJOR SCHOOL FIRES *

Loss of Life in Thirteen Major School Fires)

STRUCTURAL FEATURES FACILITATING SPREAD	CAUSE OF PANIC	CAUSE OF CASUALTIES	TYPE OF CONSTRUCTION	HEIGHT IN STORIES
Crevices in stairways Through stairways	Flame and smoke in front stairway	Door failed to open	Ordinary	3
Through stairways from basement	Flame and smoke from basement stairways	Trapped by fire and falling of girl	Ordinary	3
Wooden doors in brick Stair-tower stairways	Details not definite	Details not definite	Ordinary	4
Improvised stage and other parts	Fire on platform	One stairway from upper floor combustible	Frame	2
General	No report on panic	Burned in rooms; probably trapped in rooms	Frame	2
General	Fire in front room	Only two exits—one entirely blocked	Frame	1
General—probably stairways	Trapped by fire	Exit cut off by flames	Frame	3
Blind attic. Course indefinite	Building not occupied at time of fire	Roof collapsed killing fireman	Ordinary	3
Open spaces back of partition, corridor and stairs	Building not occupied at time of fire	Falling brick	Not reported	Not reported
Chute and spaces between floor and ceiling	No definite report	Report not definite	Ordinary	2
No definite report	Pupils were all safely removed	Reëntered to salvage clothing	Ordinary	Not reported
Probably stairway	No definite report	Exit cut off by flames	Frame	2
General	Explosion and fire	Exits ample—rapid spread of fire	Frame	1

Association. See bulletin, *School Fires*. Boston, Mass., 1931.

In later years the task of determining the degree of hazard and the minimum requirements in construction to offset these hazards has become so highly specialized that, in its detailed form, it is clearly beyond the comprehension of the average layman. Even those experts who have devoted a lifetime to the study of the problem have failed to arrive at fairly uniform conclusions. There are, nevertheless, certain prominent factors which even the layman can understand when they are presented in a simple and logical manner.

The records of school fires compiled by the National Board of Fire Underwriters and the National Fire Protection Association indicate clearly how fires started and wherein structural features and protective measures failed. The analysis of these records and the conclusions drawn therefrom should form, together with the results of research and experimental evidence, the basis for municipal building legislation.

The data presented by the National Fire Protection Association in its pamphlet *School Fires* were somewhat more detailed than the summary shown in Table 13. This table, however, serves well the purpose of calling attention to six building elements which assume major importance in the critical evaluation of present standards and requirements.

Consider first the gross structure of the thirteen buildings for which individual reports were available. All these buildings were of either frame or ordinary type construction. In the case of the ordinary schools, the reports were not specific as to the fire-resistive qualities of stairways and corridors. From the brief descriptions given, however, it is clear that the interiors in general were constructed mainly of combustible material. The Collinwood schoolhouse was considered a modern building, being representative of the average building of that time. Its heating and lighting appliances were installed according to approved methods. It is safe to assume, however, that none of these buildings would classify as standard construction today. Briefly, the conclusions to be drawn from Table 13 are as follows:

1. Frame construction, even in one-story heights, is hazardous enough to be condemned, except in temporary or emergency situations.
2. Ordinary construction without extensive fire resistance in corridors, stairways, and in partitions enclosing hazardous spaces, and without efficient fire-stopping in all walls and floors is not safe construction.
3. Poorly located or inadequate exits and stairways, and doors that fail to open, neutralize the beneficial effects of whatever

resistance is offered by construction materials to the spread of fire.

4. Panic, caused by real or apparent danger, can be positively eliminated only by the removal of all fire hazards.
5. Ordinary type buildings, exceeding one story in height, are positive fire hazards and should, under no circumstances, be used for school purposes.
6. Combustible construction in stairways and the enclosing walls of stairways and hazardous spaces are frequently the direct causes of panic and loss of life.
7. Storage of inflammable material in combustible containers or closets is a highly potential fire hazard.

The above conclusions are too well known, and they have appeared too often in recent school building standards to need further elaboration. As though in utter disregard of the plain facts revealed in the reports of school fires, and heedless of the standards recommended by educational authorities, the drafters of municipal building codes have not as yet placed a sufficiently effective ban on the construction of dangerous schools.

Reviewing in summary form the minimum requirements found in building ordinances, it was noted that (*a*) 20 per cent permitted the construction of three-story non-fire-resistive schools; (*b*) 43 per cent permitted the construction of two-story non-fire-resistive schools; (*c*) only 11 per cent insisted upon fire-resistive construction of two-story schools and 6 per cent provided for fire-resistive construction for any height; (*d*) 56 per cent are definite in their requirements for fire-resistive partitions or walls in stair hallways; (*e*) 28 per cent are positive in requiring incombustible stair carriage construction; (*f*) 36 per cent prescribe adequate protection for openings in boiler room walls; (*g*) 57 per cent were specific in prescribing incombustible walls for boiler or heater rooms; and (*h*) 18 per cent definitely prohibited the construction of storage spaces under stairways.

Of further significance is the number of these standards [26] required by each individual code. Table 14 indicates a wide range with only one code requiring standard construction for all six major features and, at the other extreme, twelve codes requiring none of these features to be of standard construction. Ap-

[26] See pages 59–60 for six standard construction features.

parently, mandatory requirements for the construction of schoolhouses as found in the ordinances of municipalities lag far behind the standards recommended by authorities. They also lack strength and extent when viewed in the light of the evidence found in the records of school fires.

TABLE 14

PER CENT OF CITY BUILDING ORDINANCES REQUIRING VARIOUS NUMBERS OF THE SIX MAJOR STANDARDS OF CONSTRUCTION

(One Hundred Cities of Different Sizes)

None	One	Two	Three	Four	Five	Six
12	16	25	24	17	5	1

Thus far the discussion has been concerned with an evaluation of building laws as measured by current school building standards. Since, as was noted in an earlier paragraph, these standards have been in vogue over a considerable period of time, it is wholly appropriate to consider seriously the need of a strengthening revision. Has the time come when, after a careful weighting of all the factors, the minimum requirement for school construction shall be fire-resistive for all heights above one story? Fire-resistive shall be interpreted to mean incombustible construction in all floors, walls, ceilings, partitions, and stairways, but with combustible materials in the finish, trim, equipment, furniture, and in certain doors not otherwise provided for. Under certain conditions it would permit combustible roof construction, if this is adequately protected from above and below.

It would be highly significant to compare the frequency and severity of fires in the various types of buildings. To be complete and reliable, such a comparison should include a fair representation of the performance of all types of construction over a uniform period of time. Unfortunately, the fire-resistive and partly fire-resistive schools are of such recent origin that a fair comparison can scarcely be made. It is significant to note, however, that in the comparatively brief time that these types have been in existence, they have contributed to the sum total of school fires. A careful inspection of Table 15 gives the impression that a fire-resistive school is no better, from the fire hazard standpoint, than a partly fire-resistive school. The text which accompanies the table explains this by noting that the number of fires in fire-resistive buildings was increased by several small and inconsequential fires in two fire-resistive technical schools. It is further noted that fires in fire-resistive buildings are a sufficient surprise to warrant mention of the type of construction in the report, whereas it is highly probable that many semi-fire-resistive buildings were reported as of brick or stone construction with wooden interiors, thereby decreasing the number of fires reported in partly fire-resistive buildings. Because of the method used in reporting the data in Table 15 it is difficult to establish the fact that the fire-resistive building is preferable to the partly fire-resistive building. There is, however, the difference between the number of reported fires in elementary and high schools, which indicates the unmistakable superiority of the fire-resistive buildings.

Authoritative opinion is by no means unanimous as to the desirability of constructing fire-resistive as opposed to partly or

TABLE 15

COMPARISON OF FREQUENCY OF FIRES IN THE VARIOUS CONSTRUCTION TYPES OF SCHOOL BUILDINGS[27]

	NUMBER OF FIRES IN:						
	High Schools	Elementary Schools	Classroom Buildings	Dormitories	Shops and Laboratories	Miscellaneous	All Schools
Brick or stone walls with wooden interior	116	151	57	73	26	29	452
Frame	25	77	15	50	9	22	198
Fire-resistive	2	0	4	4	14	10	34
Brick veneer	4	10	1	3	0	2	20
Partly fire-resistive	6	2	1	1	1	3	14
Stuccoed frame	2	1	1	1	0	1	6
Concrete block walls, wooden interior	0	3	0	1	0	1	5
No data	28	37	26	34	2	19	146
TOTAL	183	281	105	167	52	87	875

[27] National Fire Protection Association, *School Fires*, p. 44. Boston, Mass., 1931.

semi-fire-resistive schoolhouses. This division of opinion is due to a stress upon cost factors on the one hand and an emphasis on absolute safety on the other. A noted school architect argues the case for the partly fire-resistive school as follows:

> Safety is an important consideration. A law which requires all school buildings to be of fireproof construction, without regard to their size, location and general plan, is unwise and places an unnecessary handicap upon the development of schools in the smaller communities. While it is splendid practice to build school buildings of fireproof construction, and while this should be encouraged, fireproof buildings are unnecessary in small communities, if proper plans and methods of construction are employed. Of the high school population of the country, 50 per cent is found in cities of less than 8,000 population. Such communities are generally unable to provide the necessary accommodation, along with generous sites, and erect their buildings in fireproof construction throughout, within the limits of their taxing or bonding power. Such a provision, then, must needs discourage the building of new schools, and means the continued use of old, worn-out, and otherwise undesirable buildings. Where funds will not permit the erection of a fireproof building, it will require but a small additional outlay to fireproof corridors, floors, and stairways, and if the building is properly located, limited in its height, planned with due regard to circulation, stairway, and exit, and proper methods of construction are employed, it can be rendered eminently safe without the further use of fireproofing methods.[28]

Disregarding for the moment the economic factor, attention is directed toward an equally important consideration, the availability and efficiency of local fire-fighting departments. The reports of school fires show that practically all the severe fires occur in what might be classed as the small community. In three of the thirteen fires analyzed in Table 13, pages 66–67, the loss of life and property was in part attributed to the inadequacy of fire-fighting facilities. The analysis of local protection is still further evidence of the need of a serious reconsideration of what constitutes safe construction in the smaller community.

> This, with the absence of individual fire protection and total inadequacy and disability of the Collinwood Fire Department, caused the building to be totally destroyed.[29]
>
> The most noticeable fact brought out by this table[30] is the large number of cases where fire protection was inadequate or totally lacking. This was especially true of rural public and private schools and small colleges situated at a distance from a protected village or town. In some instances an attempt had

[28] William B. Ittner, "Standardization of School Buildings," *National Education Association, Addresses and Proceedings*, p. 378, 1917.

[29] National Fire Protection Association, *School Fires*, p. 5, 1931.

[30] *Ibid.*, p. 50.

been made on the part of the school to provide some sort of water supply for fire protection, but this was in many cases totally inadequate. Fire fighting facilities were often missing when there was available an adequate force of students or other people to do volunteer fire fighting. The fires show that many private school properties would have wisely spent some money on private fire fighting equipment.[31]

It seems quite paradoxical that relaxation in building requirements should be advocated for the smaller communities where the need to offset the lack of protection is greater, and that schools in larger cities should receive the beneficial effects of more effective laws and more efficient fire-fighting departments. The quotation from Ittner (page 72) stresses the economic factor as a deterrent in constructing fire-resistive schools in smaller communities. When all the facts are known, however, it may be difficult to substantiate the contention that higher initial outlays are in reality and ultimately the more expensive. Concerning only one of the elements to be considered in the situation described, namely, insurance, an authority on the subject has this to say:

Fire losses on schoolhouses have been excessive for a number of years and are steadily increasing. This means a heavy deficit, and, in consequence, an increase of rates on school property is inevitable. . . .

The record of unprotected schools is particularly bad, but even in towns with fire protection the class has been unprofitable. In fourth class towns the schoolhouse is often the largest risk, and the fire department is inadequate to cope with a fire once well started; while in towns below the fourth class the protection is negligible for a large building.[32]

Nevertheless, opinions like those expressed by the architect continue to be translated into building laws, and the laws in their turn become permissive practice in many communities. In many larger cities and in progressive and comparatively wealthy communities the local educational authorities have set their own standard, going beyond the minimum prescribed by law in their prohibition of non-fire-resistive construction in all schools above one story in height. Only seventeen of the one hundred building ordinances included in this investigation have adopted the same standard. Although no positive data are available as to the comparative prevalence of erecting fire-resistive and non-fire-resistive schoolhouses, the descriptive articles on school construction appearing in publications give the unmistakable impression that

[31] *Ibid.*, p. 50.

[32] C. C. Dominge and W. O. Lincoln, *Fire Insurance Inspection and Underwriting*, pp. 767–68.

many localities are voluntarily subscribing to the need of more protection than is offered by the law.

In justice to those who oppose mandatory legislation for the construction of fire-resistive schools it must be stated that they acknowledge the desirability of such construction, but are not yet convinced that the ultimate in safety justifies the increased costs and other sacrifices incident thereto. But the opposite view has its adherents also. Statements like the following are more commonly found in articles by and interviews with fire chiefs and inspectors.

> There is nothing to be done in dealing with school buildings but to insist upon the best fire-resisting construction, and this applies to the arrangements for lighting, heating, and storage.[33]

And there seems to be a growing disposition on the part of educational authorities to view the problem in its entirety. A school building superintendent, sensing the lessening influence of initial costs and the increasing significance of other factors, gives his opinion:

> Type A construction seems impractical for a school building. To provide fire-resistive materials for classroom floors and fire-resistive built-in furniture and equipment would involve not only an exorbitantly high cost, but it would be prejudicial to the comfort and well being of the pupils. A schoolhouse should be made safe for the youth housed therein. For this reason Type C construction, often referred to as slow burning mill construction, is not as desirable as Type B construction. Furthermore, as it has been repeatedly proved that the difference between the cost of Type B and Type C buildings is often as low as 5 per cent and seldom above 10 per cent, it is extremely unwise to attempt a saving in this direction, if for no other reason than to safeguard child life. The factors of insurance rates and maintenance charges are financial considerations which militate against any type of construction below that of Type B.
>
> *Type A.* A building constructed entirely of fire-resistive materials including its roof, windows, doors, floor and finish.
>
> *Type B.* A building of fire-resistive construction in its walls, floors, stairways, and ceilings, but with wood finish, wood or composition floor surface, and wood roof construction over fire-resistive ceiling.
>
> *Type C.* A building with masonry walls, fire-resistive corridors and stairways, but with ordinary construction otherwise, i. e., combustible floors, partitions, roofs and finish.
>
> *Type D.* A building with masonry walls, but otherwise ordinary or joist construction, and wood finish.
>
> *Type E.* A frame building constructed with wood above foundation with, or without, slate or other semi-fireproof material on roof.[34]

[33] S. G. Gamble, *A Practical Treatise on Outbreaks of Fire*, p. 454.

[34] G. F. Womrath, *Efficient Business Administration of Public Schools*, p. 120.

Published opinion of experts in the field has an undoubted value. It is based upon a large store of experience and should not be regarded too lightly. It is, however, essential to proceed a step further and reappraise the school and its hazards as they are found today. Certain real and apparent characteristics of the school building and its occupancy, as developed in Chapter II, will be applied here in the attempt to evaluate the adequacy of semi-fire-resistive as opposed to fire-resistive construction. The characteristics which have been thought of, in some instances, as reducing the hazards of the schoolhouse may be dismissed here with a brief summary of the more detailed discussion in an earlier chapter. These are:

1. Transiency of occupants.
2. Administrative variables.
3. Distribution of occupants throughout the building.
4. Hours of occupancy.
5. Internal construction.

It was clearly established that, under present systems of organization, schools accommodate a considerable number of persons at frequent intervals who may be quite unfamiliar with the various passages and stairways affording exits from the building. On this basis, therefore, the school requires a measure of protection equal to that provided by buildings in which a transient occupancy is accommodated.

While it is of utmost importance that certain administrative practices such as fire drills and housekeeping be developed to a maximum of efficiency, these practices should be considered as only supplementary to structural safety. The evidence and argument submitted in Chapter II indicate that in no sense should these practices be considered substitutes for automatic building safety.

The fire hazard in a school is not lessened in any appreciable degree by the widespread distribution of pupils, teachers, and other employees throughout the building. There is no justification for assuming that relaxation of otherwise desirable standards might be considered a result of this distribution.

The fact that the traditional school was tenanted during a fractional part of the day only and that no habitable quarters were provided within it, gave rise to a supposition that its protection might be somewhat less than would otherwise be required. The refutation of this is found in the closer analysis of the modern school and its activities. Schedules of activities in the school of today include a wide variety of school and community projects. Buildings are utilized to a much greater extent than formerly, and the evening class or meeting has become a common practice. In some sections of the country employees are permanently quartered within the school. All these factors are urgently suggestive of the need of more rather than less protection.

The factor of compulsory attendance looms large as a rather positive argument in favor of fire-resistive schools. A few thoughtful writers, having had intimate experience with the results of school fires, have had the temerity to offer this factor as a leading issue in the demand for fire-safe schools. The contrast between the school and other public and semi-public buildings in this respect is peculiarly significant. The patrons of hotels, theatres, and dwellings voluntarily assume risks that entry to these buildings entail. The school child, however, is compelled to assume the risks attendant upon his entry and stay in the school building. There is, therefore, an unescapable moral and legal obligation on the part of the community to safeguard the school child with a maximum of precautions. And it is submitted here that this obligation cannot be discharged with anything less than the safest type of building.

The subdivision of a building into comparatively small offices or rooms offers a retarding effect to the spread of fire. Firemen and insurance officials will universally maintain that hazards are greater in structures with large spaces between partitions and enclosing walls. The school, with its large classrooms and larger laboratories, study halls, and libraries, and its wide, sweeping corridors, and spacious open stairways presents a degree of fire hazard not frequently encountered in other buildings either public or private.

The quantity and combustible quality of the physical contents of school buildings, although two of the most important factors in establishing minimum safety requirements, have received comparatively little consideration in the more recent determination of these requirements. Authorities not directly associated with the process of drafting requirements and determining standards have viewed the school hazard with some alarm. The attitude of the insurance group is well represented by the quotation from Dominge (page 73). A deputy fire chief with many years of experience in the largest city in the country sums up his convictions as follows:

> In schools, hospitals, department stores the hazards are as great if not greater. [Preceding text discussed hotels, theatres and factories]. Of the entire group perhaps the schools could safely be classed as the most hazardous—especially the private school.[35]

It was noted in an earlier discussion that the non-fire-resistive schoolhouse with fire-resistive corridors and stairways was considered the minimum type of construction some fifteen or twenty years ago. The preponderance of opinion as reflected in the standards developed by school building authorities and in city ordinances has not changed materially since then. It is difficult to reconcile the attitude of the experts with the significance of the changes that have taken place with respect to the physical contents of the schoolhouse. The passage of time perpetually presents new types of hazards—new systems of lighting, heating, ventilating, and power, new processes, new operations, new materials, and new conditions; and every single one of these features may introduce not only new degrees of known hazards, but also entirely fresh elements of danger. Are these new risks compensated by a corresponding development in the introduction of safeguards? Experience gives the answer. The improvements in protection come with the realization of danger, though too often these are not generally adopted or given legal force until public indignation has been aroused over some serious loss or sad accident.

> Public apprehension, as it should, is usually aroused by calamities such as occurred at Collinwood, Ohio; Cleveland, South Carolina; and Babbs Switch, Oklahoma. Unfortunately, it seems to require some tragedy to attract public attention to the parsimony practiced in the field of creating greater fire safety in schools.[36]

A thorough analysis of the hazards of the modern school does not come within the scope of this study. It is obvious, however, to even the most casual observer that senior and junior high schools and, to a lesser but constantly increasing degree, the elementary schools are extending their programs and modifying their

[35] T. F. Dougherty and P. W. Kearney, *Fire*, p. 117.

[36] Ivan Escott, "Fire Protection for Schools," *The American School Board Journal*, Vol. 80, June 1930, p. 68.

practices in a manner that causes measurable changes in fire hazard. The implications of these trends may be illustrated by noting that certain broad principles of protection require that hazardous rooms or spaces be enclosed by fire-resistive walls, ceilings, and floors. When schools include various types of manual arts rooms, household arts departments, science units, audio-visual studios, special activities rooms, auditoriums, and whenever the comparatively non-hazardous traditional classroom is wired for various electrical services and stocked with the essential equipments of a modern program, it can mean only one safe procedure: fire-separations at such frequent intervals that the whole structure virtually becomes a fire-resistive building. It appears that all the latent potentialities for severe fires are present in the schools today—there is lacking only the inevitable incident that will awaken the public to the perils it tolerates in its schools.

2. ADEQUATE PROTECTION OF PROPERTY FROM FIRE HAZARDS

While the protection of the lives and health of the public has been held an unchallenged function of the building code, its provisions cannot legally be drafted under the present interpretation of the police power to safeguard property.

> The protection of stored commodities or prevention of interior deterioration is also an important function of walls and should be considered. It does not come within the police power.[37]

The attitude of the courts and the opinions of students of the subject are unanimous on this point. The issue will not be discussed here except to point out a rather obvious inconsistency in the application of the police power. The zoning ordinance, operating under the same constitutional public welfare clause as does the building code, admittedly seeks to conserve and promote the values inherent in both public and private property.[38] One plausible explanation of the broader powers of the zoning ordinance is in its comparatively recent introduction as a regulatory instrument. Its inception was contemporary with a significant shift in the direction of group as opposed to individual welfare. As a consequence, its authorities have been construed as applying to areas heretofore held sacred as the inalienable rights of indi-

[37] Building Code Committee, U. S. Bureau of Standards, *Recommended Minimum Requirements for Masonry Wall Construction*, p. 23.

[38] The Advisory Committee on Zoning, U. S. Bureau of Standards, *A Zoning Primer*, p. 2.

viduals. But the building code was first conceived in that period in American history when individualism was in the ascendancy and every man's home was his castle. Any code restrictions thrown about an individual's full utilization of his property could not be sustained on the grounds that public prosperity would be promoted or community property values protected thereby. And judicial opinion at present excludes property protection as a legitimate function of the building ordinance, and probably will continue to do so for a considerable period of time to come. This distinction of powers has been injected here to eliminate from the discussion any consideration of purposefully drafting local building laws so that they will effectively protect property from destruction or deterioration.

The protection of the capital investment in schools is desirable and, although mandatory measures looking toward the conservation of these values have not received judicial sanction, the building code does indirectly contribute to the dissipation or preservation of plant values. Thus, the ordinance which prescribes fire-resistive construction for schools does so solely for the purpose of providing the most effective type of protection for the occupants, but incidentally it also provides the most effective type of property protection. This fact is amply substantiated by the report of the National Association of Public School Business Officials.[39] The survey conducted by this body included sixty-five cities of various sizes located in the several geographical sections of the United States. It disclosed the fact that the amount of annual fire loss per $100 valuation on buildings of ordinary construction was more than nine times as great as that on buildings of fire-resistive construction. Unfortunately, the study did not distinguish between combustible interior and partially combustible interior ordinary construction. Nevertheless, the comparison serves to confirm common sense observation that fire losses are considerably less severe in fire-resistive buildings than they are in any type of ordinary construction. If, in making a choice between fire-resistive and partially fire-resistive construction, all other factors are held equal and constant, the protection of property factor will without question turn the decision in favor of the fire-resistive building.

[39] H. C. Roberts, "Fire and Other Insurance for Public School Property," *Proceedings of the National Association of Public School Business Officials*, p. 37, 1930.

VARIOUS COST FACTORS

In considering cost factors it seems desirable to contrast from another point of view the standards proposed by the American Institute of Architects and adopted by school building authorities, and the requirements promulgated in ordinances and recommended by building code specialists. It was noted in a previous discussion that the National Board of Fire Underwriters had recommended for legislative enactment a minimum requirement of ordinary construction with fire-resistive corridors and stairways for two-story school buildings. Other recognized code-drafting bodies have advocated substantially the same regulation. These groups, however, have been limited in their deliberations and final recommendations by legal strictures. They have not been permitted to weigh any factor except that of safety. On the other hand, school building authorities whose obligations are more extensive and whose authorities are not circumscribed by the police power of the building code have fixed upon approximately the same minimum standard. It appears that they rested their case on the same level, seemingly in disregard of the fact that it was strictly within their province to go beyond safety and weigh a number of economic, social, and educational factors, raising the minimum if the evidence so indicated. This observation is tempered by the fact that research has not yet discovered positive degrees of superiority of one type of construction over the other with respect to educational fitness, economies in construction, maintenance, and operation.

It is not the intent of this study to determine with any degree of finality the relative efficiencies of the fire-resistive as opposed to the partially fire-resistive schoolhouse. Such an analysis constitutes a major problem in itself. It is hoped, however, that by employing such evidence as is available, attention may be focused upon ultimate and total costs rather than upon the more immediate and obvious outlays. In such a tentative analysis three elements of cost will be considered: costs represented by a twenty-year equal-annual-payment serial bond issue at 5 per cent interest; insurance costs over a period of seventy-five years; and costs represented by a fire loss expectancy over a similar period of time. Other factors, though not yielding to current methods of cost analysis in the same fashion as do insurance, capital outlay, and fire loss expectancy, are none the less real. Among the more tangible of these are maintenance, operation, longevity, and educational fitness. The fire loss expectancy, although a comparable and known charge, appears to have been met, in part at least, in the payment for insurance protection. Actual comparisons of the long-time cost of the two types of construction, therefore, will be made on the bases of insurance and original outlay only.

Before continuing the discussion of the five factors not actually included in the financial comparison, it seems essential to indicate the attitude assumed by this investigation in the treatment of issues where apparent indications rather than positive evidence are the only premises. Since the argument seeks to prove the superiority of the fire-resistive building, prejudicial decisions have been studiously avoided to the extent that non-fire-resistive construction has been given the preference in doubtful issues.

In a recent and exhaustive investigation[40] of public school insurance it was discovered that the average annual fire loss per $100 valuation was $.014 for fire-resistive buildings and $.129 for non-fire-resistive buildings. This is a ratio of about 1 to 9. Insurance rates on the two types of construction, however, do not exhibit the same relationship. According to the most reliable data available, these rates throughout the country as a whole assume a proportion of about 1 to 2. This leads to the suspicion that fire-resistive buildings are being caused to carry an undue share of the insurance costs. The actuarial bureaus of the fire insurance companies have doubtless arrived at these proportional risks in a scientific way. Nevertheless, if there is any virtue at all in the statistics of the investigation reported above, the fire-resistive building is a much safer economic risk than the insurance rates seem to indicate. However, as noted above, this observation in favor of fire-resistive construction lies in that indefinite area where indications rather than absolute facts must be relied upon.

The loss in dollars and cents is not the only factor to be considered. Disruption of the educational program, the dissipation of human energy, the destruction of records and reports, expenditures for outside fire-fighting facilities—these and other social losses can scarcely be fully accounted for in the insurance indemnity. Thus, the difference in the fire losses incurred in the two types of buildings tends to become progressively greater as the

[40] H. C. Roberts, *op. cit.*, p. 37.

total situation is reviewed. Were accounting refined to the point where at least a few of these items could be isolated and translated into cost units, it would not be surprising to see the scales weighing even more heavily in favor of fire-resistive construction.

Scientific data on the relative maintenance and operation costs of the two types of construction are meagre. Such information as is available, however, indicates that maintenance charges in fire-resistive buildings are certainly not more than in non-fire-resistive buildings, and are very probably less. Schwartz[41] concluded that fire-resistive construction was, in fact, superior in this respect to lower types of construction. Operation costs will be influenced by such factors as the heat transmission properties of fire-resistive and combustible construction.

Alterations and expansions to meet changing educational and social needs seem to be accomplished with less expenditure in the fire-resistive building. Consider, for example, the classroom partition. The reinforced concrete floor slabs of the fire-resistive building will support a partition at any point, while in the non-fire-resistive building the wood floor joists will need special construction to carry the weight of a shifted partition. The units of construction comprising the various assemblies of fire-resistive buildings possess a degree of secondary utilization not equaled by those used in non-fire-resistive construction. In other words, the fire-resistive building is probably more flexible than the non-fire-resistive building. The comparative sound insulating[42] properties of fire-resistive and combustible construction should also be considered in educational fitness.

Although there have been some doubts raised as to the desirability of constructing schools with extensive life service periods, this theory has not advanced beyond the stages of tentative discussion.

> It was suggested that there would even be certain advantages in employing some form of construction for schools that had not too long a life, since great durability was of doubtful advantage. If the building were substantially cheaper in the first cost, and not seriously more expensive in maintenance, it could, it was argued, very desirably be replaced at the end of twenty-five or thirty years by a new building in conformity with the educational methods and hygienic standards of the day.[43]

[41] H. M. Schwartz, *Improvement in the Maintenance of Public School Buildings.*

[42] Donald A. Laird, "School Noises and How to Minimize Them," *The Nation's Schools*, Vol. 3, pp. 66–70, January 1929.

[43] Sir Felix Clay, *Modern School Buildings*, pp. 14–15.

A building with maximum provision for expansion and internal alteration may well be planned for an indefinite life span. In this respect there appears to be evidence of the superiority of the fire-resistive building. There is no specific authority for this assertion to be found in school building literature or research. Industry and commercial enterprise, long since concerned with the problems of depreciation, have determined the rate at which the various types of construction may be expected to deteriorate. Saliers[44] quotes the schedules of depreciation as established by various national conferences and associations. In every instance there appears to have been a longer service period assigned to the fire-resistive building. However, since the exigencies of competition and the demands for more scientific appraisal for taxation purposes have not compelled the profession of school business administration to discover true differences, the life spans for the two types of construction will be assumed equal. This policy of assuming them equal will be continued in a subsequent section where depreciation is calculated in determining the comparative insurance costs for the two types. It should be noted that the partially fire-resistive structure is again given the benefit of the doubt.

Unfortunately, there have been no extensive studies made on the differences between the unit costs of the two types of construction. Reference was had to certain isolated and fragmentary evidence which, when properly assembled and interpreted, gave some promise of yielding at least a trend, if not a definite comparison. An experiment[45] reported in *The American School Board Journal* showed that cubic-foot costs for fire-resistive construction may be as low as only 5.75 per cent more than for Type C, or partially fire-resistive construction. This experiment had the virtue of being a real situation in which bids were received on two sets of specifications for identical buildings, except that one was fire-resistive and the other partially so. Since all variables except those under comparison were held constant, it seems defensible to accept the difference of 5.75 per cent as an index of the lower limit. A well-known authority[46] expresses the conviction that the costs of fire-resistive construction may be as little as 5 per cent,

[44] Earl A. Saliers, *Depreciation—Principles and Practices*, pp. 513–14.

[45] Francis R. Scherer, "Comparative Costs of School Buildings at Rochester." *The American School Board Journal*, Vol. 68, p. 56, February 1924.

[46] G. F. Womrath, *op. cit.*, p. 120.

and seldom more than 10 per cent, more than for Type C. In a communication[47] from the technical secretary of the American Institute of Architects, the writer was informed that exact cost data of this nature were not available. Mr. Smith suggested, however, that the difference might be between 15 and 20 per cent, and based his estimate on an informal survey of fifteen fire-resistive buildings and nine non-fire-resistive and partially fire-resistive buildings. The computed average difference was 16 per cent. The investigator made a similar survey,[48] but limited the cases of non-fire-resistive buildings to those which had fire-resistive corridors and stairways. The average difference between the costs of the eight partially fire-resistive and the fourteen fire-resistive buildings was approximately 12 per cent.

The fallacy of contrasting construction costs without controlling a large number of variables is recognized, and reliability is not claimed for the differences found in the two surveys. These differences, however, assume significance when combined with other measures. In a number of informal conferences with architects and estimators, the writer was informed that differences in the costs between the two types would lie between 7 and 12 per cent. For the purpose of securing results from a controlled situation, the investigator had the cooperation of Mr. Ira H. Davey of the firm of Tooker and Marsh, Architects, New York City. The cost data sheet of a fire-resistive building completed in 1930 was used as a base. Itemized costs for wooden construction were substituted for fire-resistive materials in floors, partitions, and the roof. Corridors and stairways were left as in the original cost sheet. With all variables held constant and equal, except where the substitution was made, the difference in cost was found to be approximately 18 per cent. Since all available measures indicated that cost differences vary from 5.75 per cent at the lower limit to 18 per cent at the upper limit, it was decided to express the final comparison as a probable range.

The initial cost, then, of a fire-resistive building will probably be from 5.75 to 18 per cent more than that of a partially fire-resistive building. And when the twenty-year bond issue has been redeemed, the school district will have invested $802,600 for a

[47] Letter from Leo J. Smith, Executive Secretary of the American Institute of Architects, Washington, D. C., September 1932.

[48] In *The Architectural Forum*, Vol. 48, March 1928.

$500,000 Type C,[49] or partially fire-resistive building, and somewhere between $848,750 and $947,225 for a fire-resistive building, the contract price of which was from $528,750 to $590,000.

Since little is known about the comparative life service of the two types of construction, it was assumed, on the basis of previous investigation,[50] that each would have a service period of seventy-five years without residual value. Insurance rates were applied to 80 per cent of the values of the partially fire-resistive building, and to the low and the high estimates of the fire-resistive building. The impossibility of predicting replacement values made it necessary to use the original cost minus depreciation in calculating the insurable value. In seeking a fair average insurance rate per $100 valuation it was discovered that a large number of carefully controlled situations would have to be set up in each of the different rating sections of the country; and this in cooperation with an equally large number of rate-making bureaus. Desirable as this procedure would have been, it was obviously impossible within the scope of this study. The school building insurance studies which have been made give little information on the subject, and general insurance reports fail, in a studious way, to offer any data. It was possible, however, to arrive at a sufficiently accurate estimate through the evidence presented in the research study[51] by the National Association of Public School Business Officials, which was substantiated in part by competent authority. The research study showed that the median rate for three-year term policies on fire-resistive buildings was 26.6 cents, and for non-fire-resistive buildings, 40 cents. Insurance authorities had previously stated that these rates would show an approximate ratio of 1 to 2½. In further conference with competent authority it was decided to express the general average as a ratio of 1 to 2, with the understanding that this was a very conservative estimate, the conviction being that the non-fire-resistive type was again favored in the comparison.

A rate of $0.25 was applied to the valuations of the fire-resistive building and $0.50 to the partially fire-resistive building. In order to illustrate the striking differences that a small change in rate will cause over a long period of time, the ratio of 1 to 2½, as

[49] Incombustible stairways, corridors, and exterior walls.

[50] G. D. Strayer and R. M. Haig. *Financing Education in the State of New York*, p. 82.

[51] H. C. Roberts, *op. cit.*, p. 60, 1930.

originally suggested by insurance authorities, was also applied. Thus there were developed a series of comparisons on different estimate levels. The results are reported in Table 16.

TABLE 16

COMPARATIVE TOTAL COSTS OF TYPE C AND FIRE-RESISTIVE CONSTRUCTION OVER A SEVENTY-FIVE-YEAR PERIOD

(Based on Bond Issue and Insurance Premiums)

Cost Items	Type C Construction Cost *	Fire-Resistive Construction: Low Estimate: Cost	Low Estimate: Per cent Increase in Cost over Type C	High Estimate: Cost	High Estimate: Per cent Increase in Cost over Type C
I. Initial contract price......	$500,000	$528,000	5.75	$590,000	18.00
II. Insurance rates 50 cents per $100 on Type C, and 25 cents on fire-resistive construction †					
1. Twenty-five year equal-annual-payment serial bond issue at 5 per cent..	802,000	848,600		947,225	
2. Twenty-five three-year insurance premiums....	26,000	13,736		15,258	
Total insurance and bond issue........	828,000	862,336	4.14	962,483	16.24
III. Insurance rates at 62.5 cents per $100 on Type C and 25 cents on fire-resistive construction					
1. Twenty-year equal-annual-payment serial bond issue at 5 per cent......	802,000	848,600		947,225	
2. Twenty-five three-year insurance premiums....	32,500	13,736		15,258	
Total insurance and bond issue........	834,500	862,336	3.26	962,483	15.25
IV. Fire loss expectancy ‡......	25,125	2,850		3,237	

* Type C—Fire-resistive stairways, corridors, and exterior walls.
† Comparisons are to be made between the totals of the subdivisions II and III.
‡ The fire loss expectancy is not included in the comparisons under subdivisions II and III. It is reported in the table to indicate differences for the three estimates.

Cost differences between Type C and fire-resistive construction shrink at an unexpected rate over a long period of years. And, if by some alchemy of accounting, maintenance and operation charges, educational efficiency, and depreciation rates could be transmitted into cost units, the differences in cost would be still less. And if the fire loss expectancy were apportioned equitably, and if the true significance of this total economic loss could be extricated from insurance premiums and indemnity, there would be further decreases in the total cost differences. And finally, if sentiment permits such a proposal, should the life loss expectancy be reduced to cost units and charged against the type of construction, differences in total costs might disappear entirely. Thus, the perspective of the years and the acknowledgment of and proper accounting for all possible factors tend to extinguish differences in cost, and leave no alternative but to recommend the best and safest type of construction for schools.

Of still further significance are those factors which defy the remotest attempt at economic interpretation. It is beyond imagination to measure in currency the differences, as the two types of construction seek to satisfy the moral obligation of modern society toward its immature members. The proposition that compulsory attendance in schools imposes both legal and moral responsibilities upon society to provide the safest construction possible is another factor whose differences for the two types of construction cannot be expressed in financial terms. It would be possible to elaborate this category by drawing upon the characteristics of the school building and its occupants as developed in Chapter II. The long-term cost analysis with the references noted above, however, serves to complete the case.

Despite the facts cited in the foregoing paragraphs, the immediate burden may seem onerous to those with a view toward strict economy. The observations below indicate how recent trends may be expected in the near future to provide, without excessive initial costs to the individual community, that measure of protection which the larger and wealthier school districts have established as their minimum.

The capital outlay program for school buildings in local communities may soon become a matter of state concern. State aid which provides a minimum educational program for all localities irrespective of size, wealth, or other condition is an accomplished fact in several states. More nearly analogous to the question under discussion are the various services and aids other than education that the state is obligated to supply its various political subdivisions. Consider police protection and the various forms of relief measures. The guarantee of safety from insurrection, riot, and other internal disorders is equalized throughout the state. No rural district or village is penalized because of its size or its inability to pay for protection. When its own resources are unable to provide the measure of protection deemed desirable for the state as a whole, the state assumes a portion of the burden. Applying this well-established principle to safety from fire, the smaller community will no longer be compelled to accept risks that the larger and more fortunately situated districts are able to avoid.

Although a few municipal ordinances have already prescribed fire-resistive construction for schools two stories or more in height, and although voluntary action by municipal school building departments has, in many cases, fixed upon this minimum requirement, there are some fundamental objections to an immediate enactment of mandatory legislation of this nature. First, authorities in the field of city planning powers indicate the impossibility, for the present at least, of causing the legal requirements of building ordinances to take into account any factor except that of safety. The police power under which the code operates may not serve to protect or conserve physical values, to insure educational fitness, or to regulate according to different concepts of moral obligations. Second, mandatory legislation prescribing fire-resistive construction for all schools above one story in height may be premature and may result in serious sacrifices in other directions. School districts compelled to conform to such a law before public sentiment has been fully appraised and convinced of its desirability, may resort to such practices as building one-story buildings, or omitting essential features in order to reduce the initial cost. For these reasons, the standards recommended for inclusion in building laws have been conceived in terms of next possible steps, not in terms of the ultimate ideal. The advance proposed will mean a strengthening of practically all the city ordinances which permit two-story non-fire-resistive construction.

Out of the proposals herein stated should emerge, in due time, the ideal standard fire-resistive construction for all schools above one story in height.

The following four types of construction and the conditions that govern their acceptable uses are submitted with the recommendation that they be given legal force by their incorporation in the school building sections of local and state building codes.

Type 1. *Fire-resistive.*
Type 2. *Modified Fire-resistive.*
Type 3. *Semi-Fire-resistive.*
Type 4. *Frame.*

Type 1. Fire-resistive: Walls of masonry or reinforced concrete; structural members of incombustible material and adequately fireproofed; incombustible material in all partitions of classrooms, corridors, and stairways, and in the stair carriage, floors, and roof. Openings in exterior walls above the first story, if such openings are distant in a direct line less than thirty (30) feet from a hazardous structure, shall be protected by fire doors, fire windows, or other approved device. Interior doors or windows serving as enclosures for hazardous rooms such as manual training or paint shops, kitchens, and laboratories shall be of approved fire-resistive construction. Built-in and movable equipment, trim, furniture, and floor surfaces may be of combustible construction.

Type 2. Modified Fire-resistive: The same general construction as Fire-resistive, Type 1, except that roof construction may be of wood if properly protected on top and separated from the floors below by a fire-resistive ceiling, and that fire-resistive protection of openings in exterior walls may be omitted.

Type 3. Semi-Fire-resistive: Masonry walls, fire-resistive corridors and stairways, and completely fire-resistive basement, but with ordinary wood construction in floors, partitions, and roof.

Type 4. Frame: Wood frame construction in which the structural parts and materials are of wood or dependent upon a wood frame for support, including construction having an incombustible veneer.

Use Restrictions

Type	Permissible Locations	Permissible Heights	Maximum Undivided Floor Area	Service Period
1.	No restrictions	No restrictions	No restrictions	Indefinite
2.	Outside fire limits	No restrictions	No restrictions	Indefinite
3.	Outside fire limits	Two stories	15,000 sq. ft.	Indefinite
4.	Outside fire limits	One story	3,000 sq. ft.	Temporary

Note: Where the main first floor line is three (3) feet or more above the grade line at any entrance to or exit from any story above the basement, the basement shall be rated as the first story. Stories more than fifteen (15) feet high, measuring from the floor surface to the ceiling, shall be rated as two stories.

SUMMARY

1. Municipal building ordinances differ widely as to both extent and character of their requirements for school building construction. The majority of such ordinances fail in a conspicuous way to recognize the school as an individual structure with use and occupancy characteristics peculiarly its own.
2. Whenever municipal building legislation has isolated the school as a special case and enacted laws regulating its safe construction, there has been a marked agreement with the standards established by school building authorities. And, conversely, when the school has been conceived as another public or semi-public building and caused to conform to a series of blanket requirements for the group, there has been a distinct disagreement with current school building standards.
3. Few of the one hundred building codes studied prescribed standard safe construction for the majority of those large building features which are known, by experience, to be the most important factors in securing adequate safety.
4. Viewed in the light of progressive social ideals and appreciations, and when considered in connection with the increased hazards of the modern educational program, the school building standards of two decades ago are now approaching obsolescence.
5. Raising of standards in the past has, in a large measure, been occasioned by some tragic loss. An unreasoning faith in alleviatives rather than preventives has obstructed, in part, the deliberate anticipation of dangers from fire. Schools were built with a maximum of mitigating facilities, while fundamentals in safe construction were slighted. Periodic scientific appraisal of current and predictable future hazards, together with a searching analysis of all factors involved should be the basis for the production of standards.
6. The small community, where local fire-fighting facilities are at a minimum of efficiency, has just as great a need as the large one for fire-resistive construction in its schools, and probably greater.
7. Constitutional limitations prevent the enactment of building laws which seek to control conditions so as to bring out of them an optimum measure of building efficiency, economy, and

general adaptability to the educational program. The standards recommended by schoolhousing specialists are not thus restricted. It would be reasonable to expect that the latter would include all the safety requirements of the former plus the demonstrated needs with respect to educational fitness and economy.

8. When a long-range estimate is computed for the probable costs of fire-resistive and partially fire-resistive construction, the differences in costs tend to disappear. Other factors, although not subject to definite cost analysis, combine to weigh heavily in favor of fire-resistive construction.

CHAPTER IV

REQUIREMENTS FOR STAIRWAYS, FIRE ESCAPES, BEARING WALLS, LIVE FLOOR LOADS, AND SANITATION

STAIRWAYS

FOR the purpose of securing logical sequence and ease of reference this study includes the analysis of requirements for fire-resistance in stairways and their enclosures in the general treatment of fire-resistance in school buildings. The treatment in this section, therefore, is concerned with other phases of stairway construction in school buildings, namely, location, extent, width, and certain other dimensional characteristics. The importance of these structural features, however, is scarcely second to the need of fire-resistance in gross structure. Table 13, pages 66–67, and the quotation below indicate clearly the major significance of the part which stairways play in school fires.

> Well, the best place to begin your investigation is at the exits, for faulty exits are responsible for 65 per cent of all the life loss in school fires.[1]

Although safety is of paramount importance, there is the possibility of an ill-advised overemphasis which may result in excessive costs, poor adjustment of facilities, and unjustified conflict with the smooth administration of educational activity.

The purpose of this section will be to evaluate the adequacy of code requirements for stairways, using as measures acceptable standards, and to raise issues concerning those features on which authoritative opinion differs. Reports of experimental research are strangely lacking on this subject and, to the investigator who has studied and noted the wide variety and conflict of requirements found in building ordinances, the impression is that much of the legislation on stairways has evolved through a process of trial and error. It is not within the province of this study to conduct

[1] Alfred T. Fleming and P. W. Kearney, "Is Your School a Fire Trap?" Reprinted with permission of *The Ladies Home Journal* by the National Board of Fire Underwriters, New York, 1932.

the exhaustive field studies essential to final conclusions. In fact, some of the disputed issues resist objective treatment to such an extent that opinion evidence seems, for the present, to be the only basis for settlement. The analysis, therefore, will have recourse to such positive evidence as is available, and to the recommendations of such bodies as the National Fire Protection Association. The characteristics of school buildings, as developed in Chapter II, will also be employed wherever their application seems pertinent to stairway design. While the appraisal will seek to develop and present an analytical picture of the general status of code provisions for stairways, the more significant portion is concerned with the contrasts between blanket provisions and individual provisions for school buildings.

Determining minimum safety requirements for the number, width, extent, and location of stairways for various building occupancies constitutes one of the most difficult and elusive problems that building legislation encounters. Other factors bearing upon structural stability, such as dead and live loads, wind pressure, and the required strength of materials and assemblies to resist these forces, can be calculated with mathematical precision. But the requirements for reasonable safety in stairways in different types of buildings are so diverse, so dependent upon variables, and upon building heights, areas, and other influences, that no single formula can adequately satisfy the needs of all buildings.

The present analysis begins with a tabulation of certain requirements concerning the minimum number of stairways and their specified locations and vertical extents. It should be noted at the outset that ten ordinances failed to specify requirements that would fit into the tabulations in Tables 17 to 21. The provision cited below is the usual type of regulation found in smaller city ordinances where detailed building legislation has not been enacted.

> All buildings used as a store, factory, school, apartment, office building or lodging house and all buildings of like character shall have the number of stairs that in the judgment of the Inspector of Buildings may be required considering the class of construction and its occupancy. All such stairs shall have treads of uniform width and risers of uniform height throughout each flight and the risers shall be not more than eight inches in height and the treads, exclusive of nosing, not less than ten inches.[2]

[2] Jackson, Miss., *Building Code*, Sec. 189, p. 67, 1929.

Under such regulations the ability and integrity of the building official become practically the sole local guarantee against unscrupulous and incompetent construction, and the practice of authorizing individual opinion to make final decisions in such highly complicated structural elements as stairways seems scarcely sound. Furthermore, the need of regulation in this area is not materially influenced by the size of the city. The three-story school in the city of 10,000 population presents just as big a problem in safety engineering as does the three-story school in the city of 100,000 population. If the children attending the schools in the 100,000 to 500,000 population class of cities need the protection afforded by detailed requirements, the school children in the smaller city groups need, and are certainly entitled to, a similar degree of protection. Despite this self-evident fact there is, as Table 17 indicates, a distinct trend toward nonregulation in the smaller city groups. As was argued in the discussion on state versus local school building regulation in Chapter II, there is only one clear solution of the problem of equalizing fire protection for all the schools within the state—invest the state educational authorities with the power, and charge them with the responsibility, for drafting and administering minimum standards for the construction of school buildings.

Consensus of authoritative opinion and the recommendations of recognized standardizing bodies have fixed upon a minimum of two stairways for any area above the first floor, with an appropriate separation and an extent from the top to the bottom floor. Past experience with school fires has taught that these minimum requirements are wholly defensible. It will be noted that in those ordinances wherein the school building has been regulated under special provision there has been a marked adherence to the above standards. In contrast, however, when the school has been classified with a major class of buildings, and blanket requirements have been set up to govern stairway construction for the group as a whole, the school has suffered. Of the twenty-four codes which make special provision for the school, nineteen, or 79 per cent, require recognized standard construction. On the other hand, of the sixty-one codes which govern under blanket requirements, only thirty-six, or 59 per cent, require recognized standard practice, and the remaining codes have a range from an excessive requirement of three stairways for any area above the first floor to

TABLE 17

CODE REQUIREMENTS AS TO NUMBER, LOCATION, AND EXTENT OF STAIRWAYS IN SCHOOL BUILDINGS

(One Hundred Cities of Different Sizes)

Distribution of Cities According to Population	Number of Codes Lacking Provisions for Stairs and Stairways*	Number of Codes Requiring a Minimum of Two Stairways When Floors Exceed the Indicated Areas in Square Feet†						Number of Codes Requiring Three Stairways for Any Area	Number of Codes Lacking Definite Provision as to Number	Requirements on Separation		Requirements as to Vertical Extent		
		0	2,000	2,500	3,000	3,500	5,000			No Definite Requirements	Number with Provisions as to Separation	No Definite Requirements	Number Requiring Run from Top to Bottom	Number Requiring One or More Stairways to Roof
0– 10,000		3									3		3	1
10,000– 50,000	7	18	2	3		1	1		9	14	20	18	10	7
50,000–100,000	2	10	2	7	2			3	5	16	13	18	6	5
100,000–500,000	1	21	5		1			2	1	12	18	16	10	5
Over 500,000		3			1						4	1	2	1
TOTAL	10	55	9	10	4	1	1	5	15	42	58	55‡	31‡	19‡
National Fire Protection Association Standards for School Buildings		x									x		x	
Codes with Individual Requirements for Schools	Number Per cent	19 79%	1 4%	4 17%							13§		10§	
Codes with Blanket Requirements for Schools	Number Per cent	36 59%	8 13%	6 10%	4 6%	1 2%	1 2%	5 8%			45§		21§	19

* This column refers to Tables 17 to 21, inclusive.

† Requirements expressed in terms of pupil capacity or the number of classrooms above the second floor were reduced to square foot areas and accounted for in appropriate columns.

‡ The total of these columns will equal more than 100; 5 codes specified certain stairways to continue to the roof and others to extend from top to bottom floor, which accounts for the duplication.

§ No percentage distribution can be made when there is only one type of requirement in the column.

the utterly inadequate requirement of one stairway for an area not exceeding 5,000 square feet in the second floor. Of equal significance is the fact that nineteen of the codes with blanket requirements specify that one or more stairways must continue to the roof and terminate in some form of penthouse or bulkhead, while none of the special requirements contain such provisions. Provisions of this nature can add nothing of safety to the two- or even three-story schoolhouse but become, instead, a source of administrative difficulty and an added expense. Most of the blanket requirements which impose three stairways upon the school do so because the ordinances have associated the school with such occupancies as theatres and moving picture houses.

The poor adaptation of a general requirement to the needs of safety in a school building is illustrated in the following:

> Every building except as otherwise particularly mentioned, not more than two stories high, shall have at least one stairway not less than three feet wide, provided that such stairway is so located that no part of the second floor area shall be more than 100 feet from the stairway. In case the above requirements cannot be complied with, then such number of stairs or fire escapes shall be added so that no floor space shall be more than 100 feet from a stairway or fire escape.[3]

An explanation and brief evaluation of the prevalent methods of regulating stairway widths and numbers are essential before presenting the tabular analysis of code requirements. In pointing out the advantages and disadvantages of the several methods, certain principles have been developed as characterizing sound practice with respect to this particular phase of stairway regulation. For the purpose of avoiding lengthy repetitions the text hereinafter will use for reference the abbreviated identifications preceding each principle.

1. *Proportional distribution of stairways.* The method should distribute the service load evenly upon the required stairways under normal conditions.
2. *Additional stairways to additional load.* The method should provide for additional stairways on the basis of some fixed and definite unit of need.
3. *Adequacy of unit of need.* The method should identify the unit of need in terms of the number of individuals comprising the unit, i. e., when a certain number of rooms or certain large floor areas are used as units, there should be a code designation

[3] Fort Worth, Tex., *Building Code*, p. 35, 1928.

of the number of individuals permitted per room or the number of square feet allotted per individual.

4. *Minimum widths of required stairways.* The method should prescribe the minimum widths of required stairways.

These four principles are fundamental to this phase of stairway regulation, and no requirement can be complete without provisions covering the entire list. The incorporation of these principles in stairway ordinances will not, alone, guarantee reasonable safety. Much depends upon the detailed application of the principles. For example, the principle of additional number of stairways to additional load may be observed—but in its detailed observance the ratio may be fixed at one additional stairway to each additional 60-room unit. This is obviously a misapplication of the principle as far as schools are concerned. Consideration of the methods of direct application will be included in the latter part of this section.

The general methods employed in codes range in detail from a mere statement that there shall be good and sufficient means of egress, to complicated formulas involving empirical arithmetic weightings of several factors. The first and simplest method charges administrative discretion with the authority and responsibility of determining minimum safety requirements. Under this method the local building official must make decisions for each construction project on its own merits. The best that can be said for this method is that it embodies the ideas of flexibility and local initiative. The fact that experience has dictated the necessity for written requirements and restrictions would rule this method out as dangerous and wasteful.

A second method disposes of the problem by prescribing a minimum number of stairways, usually two, and by providing for the minimum width of these stairways. The section quoted from the Denver Ordinance is typical of this method.

(h) *School Buildings—Internal Stairways*—All public and private schools for the education of children, now built or hereafter to be built, within the City and County of Denver more than one (1) story in height, shall have not less than two (2) internal stairways, and said stairs shall be not less than five (5) feet in width, and shall not be steeper than thirty-three (33) degrees. No riser on said stairs shall be greater than seven (7) inches and no tread less than eleven (11) inches wide. Said stairs shall be provided with proper hand railings, balusters and all proper safeguards. Also one exterior incombustible stair or enclosed smoke-proof tower stair.[4]

[4] City and County of Denver, *Building Ordinance*, Sec. 203, p. 65.

In the majority of the codes which have adopted this plan there appears somewhere in the general requirements for stairways the provision that the required stairs shall be remote from each other, or that they shall be as far apart as practicable. A requirement of this nature, subject to variable interpretations, has the merit of being elastic. Rigid interpretation would insist on locating the stairways on the opposite walls of the building, while a more liberal interpretation would permit an almost promiscuous location. Thus, observance of the principle of proportional distribution is conditioned, in part, by the discretion and intelligence of local administration. The second method fails entirely to satisfy the principle of additional number of stairways to additional load ratio.

A third plan specifies minimum widths for stairways, and provides that additional stairways be included in accordance with some predetermined ratio of stairways to rooms, capacities, or floor areas. A certain number of rooms is most frequently made the basis for requiring additional stairways. The plan usually stipulates also that stairways shall be remote from each other. In some instances the maximum allowable distance of any portion of the area to be served from the nearest stairway automatically provides for additional stairways. The following extract from the Aurora Building Ordinance illustrates the combination of requirements on separation of stairways, the number of stairways to rooms, and the minimum allowable distance of any service area from the nearest stairway.

Section 903—There shall be two separate and distinct exits from each floor regardless of the height or area of the building and additional exits shall be provided to meet the following requirements:

In buildings of Type I or Type II construction one (1) exit from each floor for each one hundred (100) rooms or fraction thereof. In buildings other than Type I or Type II construction, one exit from each floor for each sixty (60) rooms or fraction thereof. In the above regulations all sleeping rooms, living rooms and dining rooms shall be included and dormitories shall be calculated as one room for each eighty (80) square feet or fraction thereof. Exits as required above may consist of combined hallways and stairways or horizontal exits from hallways. There shall not be more than seventy-five (75) feet from any room to the stairway or horizontal exit measured along hallways. The least distance between the two (2) more widely separated stairs shall be not less than fifty (50) per cent of the longest dimension of the building.[5]

[5] Aurora, Ill., *Building Ordinance*, Sec. 903, p. 25.

This requirement was written to govern a group of buildings including schools, libraries, administrative buildings, hospitals, jails, and similar structures. An additional stairway to each 60-room unit is hopelessly inadequate for schools. This provision was probably meant for buildings with small units, such as jails or hospitals. The employment of units of rooms, specified areas, or horizontal distances of service areas from stairways to secure additional exit facilities can be only an approximation. A more detailed evaluation of these devices will be presented later. The third method, then, observes the principles of proportional distribution of stairways, additional number to additional load, and minimum width, but it fails to define properly the capacity of the unit of need in terms of the number of individuals to be accommodated. In a very few isolated cases the number of square feet of floor area per individual for single types of buildings is made the basis for the calculation of additional stairway facilities. When this provision is included a refinement of regulation which has the possibilities of both economy and safety in construction is achieved.

A fourth method has the particular characteristic of providing for an increment in the aggregate widths of stairways in accordance with some fixed unit of need. A literal interpretation of requirements of this type, an illustration of which is cited below, would permit the concentration of additional exit facilities in one stairway, unless a limitation were placed on widths of individual stairways.

4. In determining the occupancy of any building, the width of stairways required for any floor area above the first floor shall be determined by the number of persons occupying such floor area, computed on the basis of fourteen persons for each 22 inches of width of stairway, plus one person for every 3 square feet of hallway floor and stairway landings in the story height of such floor, excepting that in any building where a system of automatic sprinklers is installed throughout the entire building, as required in Section 257, the number and width of stairways may be computed on the basis of twenty-one persons for each 22 inches width of stairway; and excepting that when horizontal exits are provided as required in Paragraph 2 (b) of this section, the number and widths of required stairways for floor areas above the first floor may be diminished to a basis of fifty persons for each 22 inches width of horizontal exit, provided that in no case shall there be less stairway or means of exit than required in Paragraph 3 (a) and (b) of this section.[6]

[6] City of Louisville, Ky., *Building Code*, Sec. 96, p. 75, 1926.

The intent of the foregoing regulation, however, although not specifically so stated, is to secure an even distribution of increments of width. Thus, when the floor areas exceed a certain allowable capacity for two stairways, a third stairway should be added in preference to increasing the width of the two existing stairways. When this method includes provisions for the maximum distance of service areas from stairways, the possibilities of concentration of facilities in one section are partially obviated. This plan, although it provides for graduated increases in the aggregate widths of stairways, does not provide specifically that these increases shall constitute additional stairways.

A fifth method seeks to provide adequate and additional stairway facilities by requiring that the stairs, together with the landings and hallways within the stairway enclosures, be of sufficient width in the aggregate to accommodate at one time the total capacity of the floor to be served. Note in the following quotation how this method is usually stated.

> *Section 10.22.* No stair or stairway required by this article as an exit shall have an unobstructed width of less than forty-four inches between the strings throughout its length, except that hand rails may project not more than three and one-half inches into such width. The aggregate width of stairs in any story of the building shall be such that the stairs or stairways may accommodate at one time the total number of persons ordinarily occupying or permitted to occupy the largest floor served by such stairs or stairways above the flight or flights of stairs under consideration, on the basis of one person for each full twenty-two inches of stair width and one and one-half treads on the stairs, and one person for each three and one-half square feet of floor area on the landings and halls within the stairway, provided that the number of persons to be accommodated as herein provided may be assumed at one-half of such total number of persons ordinarily occupying or permitted to occupy any floor area when the building is sprinklered and at one-third of such total number when a horizontal exit is provided in accordance with this article and at one-fourth of such total number when the building is sprinklered and a horizontal exit is provided.[7]

Attention is also directed to the omission of any requirement as to the proportional distribution of the added widths. As in the fourth method discussed, the increments may be concentrated in one or two stairways. The proportional distribution of the number of stairways is commonly provided for in the maximum allowable distance of service areas from stairways.

[7] New Rochelle, N. Y., *Building Code*, Sec. 10. 22, p. 67, 1928.

The requirement for the construction of stairways of such dimensions as will permit the accommodation of the entire capacity of the floors above the first seems to have had its origin in ordinances primarily concerned with the regulation of exit facilities in multi-storied buildings, and in buildings with comparatively sparse capacities, such as office buildings. The New York City Code has, for many years, employed this method, and it is significant that a number of cities, mostly located in the vicinity of New York City, have adopted almost verbatim the same plan. The method, without doubt, has the merits of affording the ultimate in safety, but when applied to two- or even three-story schools it seems a bit excessive.

It has been possible to explain and evaluate only the most essential characteristics of the five methods of regulating the number and widths of stairways. For the purpose of this study it was not considered essential to explain or show in tabular form the great variety of practice, inasmuch as codes seek to adopt, combine, or revise the five basic methods.

A sixth method, although used much less frequently than any of the other methods, is worthy of mention because it has been developed and recommended by the National Fire Protection Association. The framework of this plan more than its specific requirements has the characteristics of a possible solution to the problem of providing adequate yet reasonable regulation for school stairway construction. A general section on stairways prescribes Class A, Class B, and Class C stairways, each based upon the needs of certain groups of structures. In a later section, schools are considered as an individual class and, while observance of Class A construction is required, additional regulations are set up in terms of the needs of school buildings. The formula for providing additional widths is reproduced on the following page.

Other detailed requirements are too numerous to mention. This plan observes the proportional distribution of stairways principle by stipulating maximum distances of rooms from stairways; it seeks to provide additional widths of stairways by an arbitrary weighting of six different types of units of need; it provides for the minimum width of individual stairways; it fails, however, to identify the need of stairways in terms of pupil capacity.

With intelligent planning and with due regard for reasonable adjustment to varying circumstances, most of the methods dis-

Rules for Determining Required Exits

2135. *Exits from Upper Stories.* For floors above the first, stairways (or ramps, see Sec. 2136) shall be provided conforming with the preceding general requirements, in accordance with the following formula:

$$A=\frac{G\times H}{120\times B\times C\times D\times E}$$

Where

A = Number of units of stair width (one unit = 22 in.)		
B = Construction		
Ordinary	B = 4	
Fire-resistive	B = 5	
C = Protection of Vertical Openings		(All vertical openings must be protected except as requirements are modified for existing buildings by Sec. 2159.)
Open stairs	C = 2	
Enclosed stairs	C = 5	
D = Sprinkler Protection		
Unsprinklered	D = 1	
Sprinklered	D = 2	
E = Horizontal Exits		(See Section 4.)
None	E = 2	
One	E = 3	
Two or more	E = 4	
G = Gross area of each floor in square feet.		For auditorium and gymnasiums G = 6×net auditorium area. A separate calculation should be made for auditoriums and gymnasiums and exits provided accordingly, in addition to those required for the rest of the building.
H = Height of building in stories.[8]		

---

cussed in this section may be expected to produce the desired results. Dependence upon local administrative discretion is too hopeful an attutide, however. A more certain plan is needed. Given certain fundamental requisites upon which there is uniform agreement, it should be possible, through the instrumentality of experimental research, to develop a simple, workable requirement which would insure reasonable safety, and result in economy in construction and administration.

Tables 18A and 18B are companion tabulations, both being concerned with the required widths and number of stairways. In the former the categories are defined in broad enough terms to include practically all the diverse requirements found in the one hundred codes. The corresponding categories in Table 18B

[8] National Fire Protection Association, *Building Exits Code*, Sec. 2135, p. 71, 1929.

are subdivided so as to procure comparison of a more detailed nature, and are therefore limited to the recording of such requirements as would yield to classification. For example, only in rare instances did codes exhibit enough similarity in their provisions for additional stairways to justify a tabulation. This should not be interpreted to mean that codes varied widely in the results they sought, but that they differed in their methods of achieving results. Significant departures which are not revealed in the tables will be mentioned in the text.

Items of significance in Table 18A are: first, the diverse methods and combinations of methods in current use which indicate that neither experimental nor opinion evidence has as yet produced a method that meets even a majority approval; second, that comparatively few codes give special attention to the school and those that do concentrate largely on a method that provides additional stairways in an indirect way if it provides them at all; third, that more than one-half of the codes studied failed to provide specifically for additional stairways on the basis of some fixed unit of need; and, fourth, more than one-third of the codes failed to provide for either the increase in the number of stairways or the increase in the aggregate widths of stairways.

Table 18B presents the detailed specifications of the broad classifications of Columns 2 and 4 in Table 18A, and an analysis of the minimum allowable widths of individual stairways. The first category, maximum distance of areas from stairways, is divided into two columns, one recording the distances as measured from the door or exit of a room to the nearest stairway, the other recording the distance of the most remote floor area within rooms to the nearest stairway. The latter measurement is more certain to produce desired distribution of stairways since it takes into account the travel distances within rooms. In the past, when the school consisted of a series of identical units so that the distances from the most remote part of these units were nearly always equal, the former measurement may have served the purpose intended.

Another aspect of this method is concerned with the rate at which people move when leaving a building. There has been some research done on this problem, but, judging from the divers results obtained in research and the various practices as exhibited in the table, there is a need of more conclusive evidence. Consider the quotations on page 106 and note the differences.

TABLE 18A

SUMMARY OF CODE METHODS USED TO SECURE ADEQUATE WIDTHS AND NUMBER OF STAIRWAYS IN SCHOOL BUILDINGS

(One Hundred Cities of Different Sizes)

	1	2	3	4	5		6		7
DISTRIBUTION OF CITIES ACCORDING TO POPULATION	Number of Codes Providing for Additional Number of Stairways Required on the Basis of Additional Rooms, Areas, or Capacity*	Number of Codes Providing for Aggregate Widths of Stairways Governed by Capacity of Areas to Be Served†	Number of Codes Providing That Stairways Shall Be Required to Accommodate the Capacity of Areas to Be Served‡	Number of Codes Providing for the Maximum Distance of any Door of Room or Portion of Area from Nearest Stairway	Number of Codes without Provision for Additional Stairways§		Number of Codes without Provision for Either Increased Width or Additional Number of Stairways**		Total Codes
					Number	Per cent	Number	Per cent	
0– 10,000.....		2		2	1	33	1	33	3
10,000– 50,000.....	2	8	8	16	18	52	13	38	34
50,000–100,000.....	6	4	3	9	16	55	13	45	29
100,000–500,000.....	1	11	3	10	19	63	9	30	30
Over 500,000.....	2	3		1	1	25	0	0	4
TOTAL............	11	28	14	38	55	55	36	36	100
Number of Codes with Individual Provisions for Schools...	1	16	0	3					
Number of Codes with Blanket Provisions for Schools........	10	12	14	35					

* Three codes used a unit of rooms as a basis, six used square foot floor areas, two used capacity. Four of these eleven codes used the additional requirement of establishing a maximum distance of service areas from stairways, and are accounted for in Column 4 also.

† Nine of the twenty-eight codes which provided for additional aggregate widths included a provision on the maximum distance of service areas from stairways, and are accounted for in Column 4 also.

‡ Each of the fourteen codes which provided that stairways should accommodate the entire capacity included a provision on the maximum distance of service areas from stairways, and are accounted for in Column 4 also.

§ Column 5 accounts for codes which did not require additional stairways on the bases set up in Columns 1 and 4. Four codes used both methods to secure additional stairways; hence there was a total of 34 codes that provided for additional stairways. The other fifty-five codes are checked in Column 5.

**When the totals of Columns 1, 2, 3, and 4 are added to the total of Column 6, the grand total becomes 127, or 27 more codes than were included in the study. The footnotes immediately above indicate how some codes were counted twice.

TABLE 18B

CODE PROVISIONS FOR WIDTHS OF SCHOOL BUILDING STAIRWAYS AND MAXIMUM TRAVEL DISTANCES BETWEEN STAIRWAYS AND AREAS TO BE SERVED THEREBY

(One Hundred Cities of Different Sizes)

Distribution of Cities According to Population	Number of Codes Prescribing the Maximum Distance of Stairways from Areas Served*							Number of Codes Prescribing the Indicated Minimum Allowable Widths of Stairways							Number of Codes Prescribing the Indicated Minimum Aggregate Width for Each 100 Individuals Using Stairways							
	From any Portion of Floor Area				From the Door of Any Room																	
	60′	75′	100′	150′	75′	100′	125′	3′	3′4″	3′6″	3′8″	4′0″	4′6″	5′0″	12″	15″	18″	20″	22″	24″	30″	36″
0– 10,000			2						1		1				1					1		
10,000– 50,000		1	9	1	2	4	1		1	4	10	4	1			2			1	1	2	
50,000–100,000	1		2	3	2	2		2	1	7	6	1					1		1			1
100,000–500,000		1	5	2	2			1	1	5	8	8	1	1		3	2	1	1			
Over 500,000					1							3		1		2		1				
TOTAL......	1	2	18	6	7	6	1	3	4	16	25	16	2	2	1	7	3	2	3	3	2	1
Number of Codes with Individual Provisions for Schools...			1		3					4	1	10	2	2		6	2	1	3			1
Number of Codes with Blanket Provisions for Schools......	1	2	17	6	4	6	1	3	4	12	24	6			1	1	1	1		3	2	

Note: Sixty-two codes omitted requirement on maximum distance of any floor area from the nearest stairway; thirty-two codes omitted requirements on widths of stairways; seventy-two omitted requirements on aggregate widths of stairways.

* Three codes gave distances both from door of rooms and from the most remote floor areas, thereby bringing the total to 41, three more than the total in Column 4 of Table 18A.

Egress Data I were made up from the first draft made by the committee on safety to life and applied to the Rochester schools. There was a question as to whether 45, 60, or 75 pupils could pass through an exit unit in one minute. We discovered from actual experience that under proper training and favorable conditions, it was possible to have 75 pupils pass a given point in one minute. In nearly every school, 60 pupils could pass a given point in one minute, but in a few schools this number was reduced to 50. It was decided, therefore, by the committee that it would be safe to fix this number at 45, and, I believe, it has remained the same ever since although many other changes have been made in the rules.[9]

In the calculation of the effectiveness of stairs and exits in schools, theatres and places of public assembly, it shall be considered that 30 persons per minute may pass down each 22 inches of width of stairs, and that 50 persons per minute may pass through each 22 inches of width of horizontal exit. People moving in a horizontal direction are assumed to move at the rate of 200 feet per minute, and when moving down stairs or inclines, come down vertically at the rate of 100 feet per minute. For the calculation of the number and width of stairs required for any floor, add the number of people on the floor in question to the number occupying the floor above.[10]

Stairways should be sufficient in number to empty the building in three minutes or less, the basis of actual determination for each building being the rule that 120 pupils in line, two abreast, can pass a given point in one minute.[11]

The section from the San Diego, California, Code is significant in that it recognizes the difference between the rates of movement in horizontal and vertical directions. A critical evaluation of any one of the three quotations must await further investigation. Only three codes (one specified distance under both subdivisions) made special provision for the school by specifying maximum distances from areas to stairways. It is possible only to speculate upon the reluctance of code-drafting bodies to use this measure when schools are under consideration. Their actions, as reflected in the codes, may indicate a hesitance to use inconclusive data, to recognize a markedly different need in the schools, or to depart from simpler methods. This much is certain, however, that when requirements on maximum distances between the most remote areas and the nearest stairway or exit range from 60 to 150 feet, and that when maximum distances between doors of rooms and the nearest stairway or exit range from 75 to 125 feet, there is an urgent need of a scientific determination of true demands on egress facilities.

[9] Letter from Mr. J. M. Tracy, Superintendent of School Buildings, Rochester, N. Y., March 1932. [10] San Diego, Calif., *Building Code*, Sec. 212, p. 104, 1930.
[11] N. L. Engelhardt, *Standards for Junior High School Buildings*, p. 45.

In the second category of Table 18B, "Minimum Allowable Widths of Stairways," more diversities are encountered. The most significant point is the wide variance between the individual and blanket requirements for schools. Judged by the standards of school building authorities, the blanket requirements are failing in a most conspicuous way to recognize the characteristics of the school occupancy.

In the third category the unit of aggregate width for each one hundred individuals using the stairways ranges from 12 to 36 inches. The unit of width here is presumably based upon the space normally occupied by an individual as he progresses. For the school as an individual building, the most frequent unit was 15 inches. It would be significant to determine the degree of safety sacrificed at the lower limit and the economies in construction sacrificed at the upper limit. However, the spread is once again of such proportions that, if this method is worthy of continued use, steps should be taken by responsible bodies to bring about a more uniform practice based upon sound evidence.

In the analysis of stairways thus far there has been reference to the lack of a scientific definition of the need of both the initial minimum and the graduated increases in stairway facilities. In this connection, it will be recalled that one of the four fundamental requisites[12] of sound stairway regulation demands that all units of need be expressed in terms of their actual service load, not in such approximations as rooms or large aggregate areas. In the observance of this principle it becomes necessary, then, to write stairway requirements so that facilities will be provided according to the number of children who will use them. There have, however, been no very significant attempts by code-drafting bodies to ascertain the true capacities of school buildings in this way. And when the extremes, as illustrated by the requirements for three separate stairways for the least area above the first floor on the one hand, and one stairway for areas up to 5,000 square feet above the first floor on the other, are noted, regulation seems to have missed its purpose entirely. Other ordinances exhibit a tendency to recognize the pupil station as the final measure, but their definitions of these stations vary from 15 to 25 square feet.

For the purpose of determining the number of occupants in any floor area of a building, unless information is furnished giving a more accurate determina-

[12] See pages 96–97.

tion, the following assumptions will be made as to the floor area occupied by each individual. . . .

2. Fifteen (15) square feet in schools, colleges, court rooms and restaurants.[13]

When the number of persons to be accommodated by the exits is not stated in the application for a permit to construct, such number of persons within any floor area shall be taken, according to the use of such floor area as one person:

(b)—For every twenty-five (25) square feet in court rooms, restaurants and classrooms in schools and colleges.[14]

It is quite impossible to determine in advance an average per-pupil floor area for all types of schools. It seems futile, if not dangerous, to specify a fixed number of square feet per pupil when the nature of the educational activity may call for a minimum of 15 square feet in classrooms to 30 or more in gymnasiums and laboratories.

It is a characteristic of the school that its varied program resists any attempt to fix upon it those inflexible requirements which are suited to other buildings wherein the congregation of individuals varies but little in numbers from room to room. If, in the promulgation of building ordinances, it is necessary to include specific per-pupil areas, adequate standards[15] for the various types of rooms should be employed.

In concluding the discussion of Table 18B attention is again directed to the outstanding fact that only a comparatively small number of building ordinances contain special provisions for the minimum widths and required increases in width of school building stairways, and that blanket provisions, seeking to control a widely diversified occupancy, have failed notably to take into account the peculiar characteristics of the school with respect to internal structure, use, and physical stature of occupants.

The facts revealed in Table 19 continue the pronounced trends shown in Tables 18A and 18B. The individual requirements for school buildings are almost in entire accord with the standards of school building authorities. Engelhardt[16] recommends a 10- to 12-inch tread and a 6- to 7-inch riser, and the National Fire Protection Association[17] advocates a maximum rise of 7 inches and a 10½-inch minimum width of tread. Grouping the school build-

[13] Mount Vernon, N. Y., *Building Code*, Sec. 2, p. 23.

[14] New Orleans, La., *Building, Electrical, and Plumbing Code*, Sec. 67, p. 101.

[15] George D. Strayer and N. L. Engelhardt, *School Building Standards*.

[16] N. L. Engelhardt, *Standards for Junior High School Buildings*, p. 49.

[17] National Fire Protection Association, *op. cit.*, p. 11.

TABLE 19

CODE PROVISIONS FOR THE WIDTHS OF TREADS AND HEIGHTS OF RISERS OF REQUIRED STAIRS IN SCHOOL BUILDINGS

(One Hundred Cities of Different Sizes)

DISTRIBUTION OF CITIES ACCORDING TO POPULATION	NUMBER OF CODES PRESCRIBING THE INDICATED MAXIMUM HEIGHT OF RISERS								NUMBER OF CODES PRESCRIBING THE INDICATED MAXIMUM WIDTH OF TREAD					
	6″	6½″	6¾″	7″	7¼″	7½″	7¾″	8″	9″	9½″	10″	10½″	11″	11½″
0– 10,000					2					2				
10,000– 50,000	1	1				1	12	3		13	3		1	1
50,000–100,000		2		1		6	7	10	8	6	4	1	2	
100,000–500,000	1	1	1	4	1	2	5	2	1	7	6	2	2	
Over 500,000				2			1		1	1		1		
TOTAL	2	4	1	7	3	9	25	15	10	29	13	4	5	1
Number with Individual Requirements for Schools	2	4	1	4		2			1		3	2	5	1
Number with Blanket Requirements for Schools				3	3	7	25	15	9	29	10	2		

Note: Thirty-four codes did not provide for heights of risers. Thirty-eight did not provide for widths of treads.

ing with other public or semi-public buildings for purposes of securing appropriate heights of risers and widths of treads results in a positive denial of the diversified needs of different age groups.

The heights of single flights of stairs have been limited by ordinance, for the purpose of securing safety and comfort. In Table 20 the practices of municipal building regulations with respect to the allowable heights of stair flights are recorded. Again the wide diversity of requirement is strongly suggestive of the tentative status of stairway regulation. And the special requirements for schools are so few that no generalization is possible, except to conclude that special requirement is not essential, or that code writers, failing to appreciate the needs of the schools, evade the problem. There have been standards established for school buildings, but the individual requirements noted in the table fail markedly to agree with these standards. The National Fire Protection Association[18] recommends a maximum height of ten feet, and the National Board of Fire Underwriters[19] advocates a maximum of eight feet. Under the latter standards it becomes imperative to break a run of stairs between two stories, while all but one of the individual code requirements permit the unbroken flight of stairs from story to story. It is obvious that the long flight of stairs without the ample landing to afford pause for rest or physical adjustment invites discomfort in normal use and danger in emergencies.

The landings between stair flights have received more attention in regulation than have the extents of continuous stairs. Widths and lengths of landings, unless properly proportioned with respect to the stairs they serve, become potential sources of danger, especially in emergencies. The deviation of the requirements from recommended practice is not great enough to warrant extensive comment. The National Board of Fire Underwriters[20] recommends that the length and width of landings be not less than the width of the stairs. The National Fire Protection Association[21] recommends a landing length of at least four feet, but omits mention of required width. It is significant, however, to note the degree of uniformity exhibited in the requirements with respect to the width of landings, and the diversity in requirements with re-

[18] The National Fire Protection Association, *op. cit.*, p. 11.

[19] National Board of Fire Underwriters, *Building Code*, p. 60, 1931.

[20] *Ibid.*

[21] National Fire Protection Association, *op. cit.*, p. 11.

TABLE 20

Code Requirements for Heights of Stair Flights Between Landings, and Dimensions of Landings in School Buildings

(One Hundred Cities of Different Sizes)

Distribution of Cities According to Population	Number of Codes Prescribing the Indicated Maximum Height of Single Flight of Stairs													Number of Codes Prescribing the Indicated Minimum Dimensions for Stair Landings				
	Expressed in feet							Expressed in risers						Width	Length			
	8	10	11	12	13	13½	16	12	15	16	17	18	20	Same as Stairs	Same as Stairs	3′	3½′	4′
0– 10,000		1																
10,000– 50,000	6	2		2	3	2			1			1	1	8	3	4	2	1
50,000–100,000	3	1	4	3	1					1	3	1		5	1	2	1	
100,000–500,000	4	4		2		2	3	1		2	2			11	4	3		4
Over 500,000						1						1	1	2	2		1	
Total	13	8	4	7	4	5	3	1	1	3	5	3	2	26	10	9	4	5
Number with Individual Provisions for Schools	1	1			2	3	3			1	1			9	4		1	3
Number with Blanket Provisions for Schools	12	7	4	7	2	2		1	1	2	4	3	2	15	6	9	3	2

Note: Forty-one codes had no requirements on heights of single flights. Forty-six had no requirements on dimensions of landings.

spect to length of landings. In the former the width is obviously governed by the width of the stairs; in the latter, however, no such fixed point of reference is available.

The salient point brought out by Table 21 is a further emphasis on the diversity of practice revealed in preceding tabulations. Specifically, the table indicates that a surprisingly large number of ordinances fail to insist upon handrails and emergency lighting on stairways. These features are considered indispensable by school building authorities and other recognized standardizing agencies. It is significant to note the very few ordinances which make individual provision for the heights of handrails and for the inclusion of intermediate rails for schools. Only one of the one hundred codes studied specified the height of handrails on school stairways. None of the model codes prepared by standardizing agencies mentioned the matter of height. It is difficult to see any relationship among the purposes of requirements which differ so widely as do those on center handrails. It would seem a comparatively simple matter to arrive at a certain stairway width, so that when it is divided by a handrail in the middle, the space on either side will be in multiples of the unit width required by the age group using the stairway. For example, the most commonly specified width requiring a center handrail is seven feet. This leaves an unobstructed width of three feet, six inches on each side, a space which, in the interests of economy, comfort, and safety, should permit the easy passage of lines of pupils two abreast. But, since both actual practice and recommended practice have failed to agree on the unit of width for one line of pupils, it is hardly expected to find a basis for agreement in this related matter.

The requirement for headroom does not become a serious consideration in average stairway construction. But when it is desired to run a pair of stairways, one for descending and the other for ascending traffic, through the same stair hallway the minimum height of seven feet will make necessary a greater story height throughout the building than would otherwise be required. The flight of descending stairs in the arrangement is located just above the ascending flight so that, under the average permissible or recommended story height for schools, the clearance between the treads of ascending stairs and the soffits of descending stairs will be less than seven feet.

TABLE 21

CODE REQUIREMENTS FOR HANDRAILS, HEADROOM, AND EMERGENCY LIGHTING ON STAIRWAYS IN SCHOOL BUILDINGS

(One Hundred Cities of Different Sizes)

DISTRIBUTION OF CITIES ACCORDING TO POPULATION	NUMBER OF CODES REQUIRING HANDRAILS ON BOTH SIDES	NUMBER OF CODES REQUIRING THE INDICATED HEIGHTS OF HANDRAILS				NUMBER OF CODES PRESCRIBING THE MAXIMUM WIDTH OF STAIRWAY WITHOUT MIDDLE RAIL							NUMBER OF CODES PRESCRIBING THE INDICATED MINIMUM HEADROOM		NUMBER OF CODES REQUIRING EMERGENCY LIGHTING IN STAIRWAYS
		2′ 6″	2′ 7″	2′ 10″	3′ 0″	5′ 6″	6′ 0″	6′ 6″	7′ 0″	7′4″	8′ 0″	9′ 10″	6′ 9″	7′	
0— 10,000															
10,000— 50,000	19	2			1			1	6	3	2		1	2	8
50,000—100,000	17	4			1	1	1		7	1	2			3	7
100,000—500,000	19	3	1	1		1	2	1	8	1	1	2		2	9
Over 500,000	4	1					1					1			2
TOTAL	59	10	1	1	2	2	4	2	21	5	5	3	1	7	26
Number with Individual Provisions for Schools	12	1					4				1	2			1
Number with Blanket Provisions for Schools	47	9	1	1	2	2		2	21	5	4	1	1	7	25

Note: Forty-one codes do not require rails on both sides of stairways; forty-five of the fifty-nine provisions on handrails fail to specify required heights; fifty-eight codes fail to specify requirements for center handrails; ninety-two codes fail to specify requirements for headroom; seventy-four codes fail to specify requirements for emergency lighting.

FIRE ESCAPES

Outside fire escapes are safety measures which have been much favored in state and local legislation. The visible effects of such legislation and the confidence it begets in the public are to be seen clinging to the exterior walls of school buildings throughout the country. The original purpose of such devices was to supply an emergency means of escape in that period of building development before the enclosed fire-resistive stairway and corridor had been conceived of as superior means of escape. The reasons for their continuance on the statutes and ordinances might be ascribed to an ill-advised economy, to a false sense of security, to tradition, or to mere imitation. And the alleged lobbying of manufacturing interests has also been charged with preserving this profitable market in fire escapes. Interesting as the speculation on these reasons might be, the all-important fact is that the exterior fire escape in all its varied forms seems to be a self-perpetuating construction feature. How it has resisted the combined attacks of educational authorities, safety engineers, fire chiefs, and other qualified experts is a mystery.

> The fatuous faith of the majority of school authorities and laymen in the life saving power of outside fire escapes is a constant source of wonder and pain to the student of fire protection.[22]

> Fire escapes, though required by law in many states, should not be found upon school buildings designed for the highest degree of safety unless they are planned as inclosed stairways and the pupils are required to use them at least once a day.[23]

> The inclosed stairway or "interior fire escape" is one that can stand a great deal of emphasis, for we still place too much faith in those old-fashioned iron escapes on the outside of buildings. Hundreds of people have died on them in jams that resulted from somebody's falling on the steep and difficult ladders, others have been trapped by flames from windows below.[24]

Lest this indictment of the fire escape may seem too harsh, acknowledgment is made of the useful purpose it served in its day. Probably a far greater number of people have been saved by it than have perished because of it. But latter-day experiences, as summed up in the quotations above, indicate that when efficiency, economy, and safety are all considered, the preference should be

[22] H. W. Forester, "Fire Protection for the Schools," *The American Architect*, Vol. 117, Pt. III, pp. 323–26, March 10, 1920. [23] William B. Ittner, "Standardization of School Buildings." *National Education Association, Addresses and Proceedings*, pp. 375–79, 1917. [24] T. F. Dougherty and P. W. Kearney, *Fire*, p. 120.

for the interior fire-resistive stairway. Additional, although of minor importance as compared to safety, are those considerations discussed in Chapter II. Nothing else detracts from the pleasing appearance of a school building so much as does the skeleton framework of a rusty iron fire escape. Numerous and varied difficulties in the administration of the routine school day can also be charged to the fire escape. From his practically unlimited store of anecdotes an eminent authority told the writer of the case where he found, in a non-fire-resistive school, the door to the spiral fire escape nailed shut. Upon inquiring, he learned that this had been done to prevent children and others from entering or leaving the school at unauthorized times. How often the fire escape has been directly responsible for acts of mischief, vandalism, and even burglary can only be conjectured.

The investigator experienced more difficulty in the interpretation of code requirements for fire escapes than of those for any other building feature except auditoriums. It was impossible, for example, to distinguish in many instances the difference between those provisions which related to old and new construction.

Frequently the wording of the requirements was vague—as though the drafters had deliberately evaded the issue, preferring to pass the responsibility on rather than to commit themselves to a positive denial or approval. The two quotations below illustrate the evasive character of these requirements. It should be noted particularly that neither of them expressly prohibits or requires fire escapes.

> One of these (required) means of exit may be served by a smokeproof tower or an exterior fire escape if approved by the Building Inspector and Fire Marshal.[25]

> All buildings now existing or hereafter erected shall be provided with good, safe and sufficient means of egress in case of fire or panic.
>
> Such means of egress from floors not at grade shall be by means of opened or enclosed service stairways, fireproof tower stairways, fire escapes, fire escape ladders through adjoining buildings or other equivalent means approved by the Building Inspector.[26]

The first quotation is identical in intent with the requirements of the twenty-six codes accounted for in Table 22 under the category "Number of Codes Permitting Substitution of Fire Escapes for One Interior Required Stairway," and the second is identical

[25] Tacoma, Wash., *Building Code*, Sec. 54, p. 54, 1924.
[26] Sioux City, Iowa, *Building Code*, Sec. 300, p. 149, 1921.

in intent with those accounted for under "Number of Codes Permitting Fire Escapes."

Thirty-four of the one hundred codes either failed to mention fire escapes, or included provisions for them in such language that the intent of the drafters could not be interpreted. This occurred usually when there was a section on interior stairways which specified a full complement of means of egress without including the fire escape. Apparently the intent in these sections was to bar the fire escape. Later, usually toward the end of the code, there would be a separate section on fire escapes, totally unrelated to the former section on stairways and, in many instances, contradictory to it. It may be asserted with confidence that the total omission of the fire escape from egress requirements means effective disapproval. But it is impossible to guess the intent of contradictory or vague requirements.

The significant facts in Table 22 are that only six codes effectively disapprove fire escapes and that twenty-three codes definitely require them. The legal priority of state legislation is doubtless responsible in many instances for the retention in local ordinances of the outside fire escape either as a permissive or a required feature. Several codes either referred to the state law or quoted from it, as illustrated below.

(a) *Fire Escapes.* Outside metal fire escapes must be provided for all buildings more than two stories in height—see State Law, C. S. 6081–6087.

When requirements for stairways are met and where this does not conflict with the State Law outside fire escapes may be omitted.[27]

The lower portion of Table 22 reveals a situation similar to that shown in previous tables with respect to the comparison of individual requirements. The important fact is that the individual requirements tended to be definite as to the inclusion or exclusion of the fire escape. When the school was governed under blanket requirements the reverse was true. Of special interest is the fact that only one of the one hundred codes specifically prohibited fire escapes on schools as an individual class of buildings.

LIVE LOADS

In the construction of schools and other types of buildings care must be exercised in the design of walls, floors, and other assemblies so that they will bear safely all superimposed loads. The

[27] North Carolina, *Building Code*, Sec. 1, p. 32, 1930.

TABLE 22

CODE REQUIREMENTS FOR EXTERIOR FIRE ESCAPES FOR NEW SCHOOL BUILDING CONSTRUCTION *

(One Hundred Cities of Different Sizes)

	PROHIBITIONS	SANCTIONS			
DISTRIBUTION OF CITIES ACCORDING TO POPULATION	Number of Codes Specifically Prohibiting Fire Escapes on New Construction	Number of Codes Permitting Substitution of Fire Escapes for One Interior Required Stairway	Number of Codes Requiring Fire Escapes †	Number of Codes Permitting Fire Escapes	Total Number of Codes Indefinite or without Provisions
0– 10,000					3
10,000– 50,000	3	9	8	2	12
50,000–100,000		10	7	4	8
100,000–500,000	2	7	6	5	10
Over 500,000	1		2		1
TOTAL	6	26	23	11	34
Number with Individual Provisions for Schools	1	3	12		
Number with Blanket Provisions for Schools	5	23	11	11	

Note: A few of the codes made story heights the basis for requirements.

* Tabulation does not include exterior enclosed stairs or fire towers.

† No distinction was made in the codes between fire-resistive and non-fire-resistive buildings.

accurate determination of the strength of various materials and combinations of materials to withstand stated amounts of pressure, thrusts, and loads is a technical problem which will not be discussed in this study. Consideration of the live load occasioned by the character of the activity of the occupants is, however, both vital and pertinent.

The United States Bureau of Standards defines the dead and live load and distinguishes between them as follows:

Dead load—The dead load in a building includes the weight of all the walls, permanent partitions, framing, floors, roofs, and all other permanent stationary construction entering into a building. (See Appendix, par. 16, for weights of materials.)

Live load—The live load includes all loads except dead loads.[28]

The live load for any floor of a school will consist of the combined weight of the maximum anticipated human occupancy, desks, and equipment, plus an arbitrarily fixed weight to give a factor of safety beyond that actually anticipated. It is probably this margin of safety that has caused much of the variation found in the code requirements today. In the earlier history of building regulation, before scientific experimentation had been invoked as an aid in determining reasonable standards, these loads were naturally assumed to be much higher than was required for safety. In the exhaustive investigation by the Building Code Committee of the United States Bureau of Standards in 1923 a totally unwarranted variation of floor load requirements was found in local ordinances. Commenting upon this condition, the Committee says:

> It was found that live loads assumed in designing many types of buildings were largely matters of tradition and had scant scientific basis. The result was that the accuracy in stress computations was defeated because of ignorance of the loads causing stresses. The building professions for years have busied themselves with tests of materials, but have given little attention to this complementary factor of loads.[29]

Although it would seem to be a simple matter to determine quite accurately the load that any particular type of floor might be required to sustain, there have been few published reports of authentic experiments. E. H. Enger[30], architectural engineer of the Bureau of Buildings, Minneapolis Board of Education, caused a test to be made in 1920. In a room 24 feet 5 inches by 32 feet (781.3 square feet) 258 pupils were placed. This gave 3.03 square feet of floor per pupil, including space taken by desks. The room was crowded, two pupils in each seat, aisles and all other spaces filled. The total live load under this condition was 41.7 pounds per square foot. Under normal utilization, forty-eight pupils and the teacher, the load was 10.83 pounds per square foot.

[28] Building Code Committee, *Minimum Live Loads Allowable for Use in Design of Buildings*, p. 5.

[29] *Ibid.*, pp. 1–2.

[30] E. H. Enger, "Test Shows Actual Live Load on School Room Floor," *Engineering News-Record*, Vol. 84, p. 924, May 6, 1920.

A later investigation by Stineman [31] found the maximum possible load on a classroom floor to be 28 pounds per square foot. He assumed a classroom of 736 square feet with two adults in each seat and thirty more standing in the open spaces next to the walls. As a result, he concluded that a requirement of 75 pounds per square foot is excessive.

The Building Code Committee [32] of the United States Bureau of Standards has established a minimum live load of 50 pounds per square foot for classrooms with fixed seats and a minimum live load of 100 pounds for corridors, stairways, gymnasiums, and assembly halls without fixed seats. This latter recommendation does not specifically mention schools, but the intent is clearly to include such occupancies.

The reports of these experiments and the recommendations of the Building Code Committee provide reliable data for the guidance of code writers up to a certain point. It should be noted that the experiment by Enger assumed a crowded condition that is seldom, if ever, encountered in the occupancy of a school. Stineman assumed a condition that is not infrequent, as adults attend entertainments, exhibits, and meetings of various types in schools. The Code Committee specifies a minimum load without reference to any degree of occupancy, the assumption being that all possible loading conditions will be adequately met. It is singular, however, that none of the three reports recognize and provide specifically for the loading of the classroom floor which is planned for movable furniture. Whether the Code Committee's standard of 100 pounds for assemblies without fixed seats applies to a classroom without fixed seats is open to question.

Fixed seating is assumed to limit the capacity of a floor to a lower maximum utilization than does movable seating. The assumption here is most important in the structural design and the planned use of school classrooms. If a local code prescribes a minimum floor load for classrooms with fixed seats, and floors are built accordingly, there are three possible results, none of which are satisfactory: first, fixed seating becomes a permanent condition and flexibility to permit change in harmony with progressive methods in education is lost; second, requirements may

[31] Norman M. Stineman, "Excessive Floor Loads Specified for School Buildings," *The American Architect*, Vol. 123, pp. 334–35, April 11, 1923.

[32] Building Code Committee, *op. cit.*, p. 5.

be disregarded in later use with a chance of overloading and subsequent risk of failure or collapse; and, third, requirements for fixed seating may be set at a level sufficiently high to insure safety for movable seating. It appears, therefore, that although much progress has been made toward a standardization of loading requirements, there is still no definite experimental evidence as to the maximum loading of a classroom floor without fixed seats. The extreme loading employed by Enger, described in a preceding paragraph, approaches the maximum possible loading of any classroom floor either with or without fixed seating, provided the room is not converted into a storage space. It is within the range of possibility, and experience confirms it, that classrooms may, while open to the public for civic, social, or educational purposes, be subjected to heavy loading which may exceed even the conditions of Enger's experiment.

The variations in live load requirements, as noted in Tables 23 and 24, range from a dangerously low level to an exceedingly high level. In the absence of definite knowledge as to the probable demands on the strength of floors it is unquestionably better to err on the side of safety, and this is what appears to have happened in local building ordinances. Thus, only eight of the sixty-four codes [33] specifying floor loads for classrooms set the minimum at 40 pounds per square foot, 10 pounds less than recommended by the United States Bureau of Standards, while thirty of them exceed this recommendation, eighteen of them by more than 20 pounds per square foot. This trend is observed in the minimum live load requirements for other types of school floors, the ratio of the low to the high in some instances being as one to more than three.

Before any further comparisons or criticisms can be made it is essential to point out that the categories, "Fixed Seats," "Movable Seats," and "Seating Not Specified," do not include data that can, in the close analysis, be combined to give a total average. The variations between the averages for the three categories, as shown in Columns 3, 6, and 9 in Table 23, indicate clearly that code writers recognized differences although the bases for these differences have not yet been clearly established. The low average of 54.5 pounds per square foot for "Fixed Seats" and the higher average of 73.8 pounds per square foot for "Movable

[33] Excludes requirements for movable seating.

TABLE 23

CODE REQUIREMENTS FOR MINIMUM LIVE FLOOR LOADS (EXPRESSED IN POUNDS PER SQUARE FOOT) ALLOWED AS A BASIS OF STRUCTURAL DESIGN FOR CLASSROOMS AND AUDITORIUMS

(*One Hundred Cities of Different Sizes*)

Distribution of Cities According to Size	Total Number of Requirements	Total Average Load	Fixed Seats			Movable Seats			Seating not Specified			Number of Codes Without Requirements
			Average Load	Number of Requirements	Range	Average Load	Number of Requirements	Range	Average Load	Number of Requirements	Range	
	1	2	3	4	5	6	7	8	9	10	11	12
Classrooms												
0– 10,000												
10,000– 50,000	22	63.6	50.0	4	50	86.7	3	60–100	62.7	15	40–100	3
50,000–100,000	23	63.9	52.9	7	50–60	66.2	4	60–75	69.6	12‡	40–150	15
100,000–500,000	27	56.9	55.7	7	40–75	62.0	5	60–70	55.7	15	40–75	10
Over 500,000	5	88.0	75.0	1	75	125.0	1	125	55.0	3	40–75	8
TOTAL	77*	61.9	54.5	19	40–75	73.8	13	60–125	61.7	45	40–150	36
United States Bureau of Standards Survey, 1923	96†	69.0							69.0	96	40–150	
Auditoriums												
0– 10,000												
10,000– 50,000	18	92.8	78.3	3	75–80	105.0	4	100–120	101.4	11	60–125	3
50,000–100,000	19	89.7	65.7	7	50–100	103.6	7	100–125	104.0	5	100–120	15
100,000–500,000	30	93.3	73.3	9	50–90	103.6	11	100–120	99.5	10	75–125	17
Over 500,000	5	95.0	75.0	1	–75	125.0	1	–125	91.7	3	75–100	9
TOTAL	72	93.7	71.5	20	50–100	104.8	23	100–125	100.2	29	60–125	47
United States Bureau of Standards Survey, 1923			95.9	102§	50–100	110.3	102§	70–150	99.5	101**	60–150	
Number with Individual Requirements for Schools	30	96.3	75.0	3		106.2	4		97.4	23		
Number with Blanket Requirements for Schools	42	91.7	70.9	17		104.5	19		110.8	6		

* Includes 64 codes, 13 of them having requirements for both fixed and movable seating.
† Includes 96 codes, no reference to seating. Comparison is therefore most valid under the column, "Seating Not Specified."
‡ Includes one blanket requirement of 150 pounds. § Assembly halls in general. ** Individual requirement for schools.
Note: Minimum safety requirements for classrooms, 50 pounds; auditoriums with movable seats, 100 pounds; authority, U. S. Bureau of Standards.

Seats" indicates a real distinction between these two categories. The average of 61.7 pounds per square foot for "Seating Not Specified," being vague as to the inclusion or exclusion of the other two types, may be interpreted and applied as the situation may demand. Whether the loss in definiteness is compensated by the gain in flexibility is open to question. The average of 61.7 pounds per square foot is undoubtedly excessive for fixed seating, and indications are that it is not high enough for movable seating. Nevertheless, more than two-thirds of the requirements were written without reference to any particular type of seating.

The average minimum load requirements for the three types of seating, although made up of slightly dissimilar elements, serve to give a sufficiently accurate composite of the total situation, and provide bases for comparison. Since the average of 69.0 pounds per square foot reported in the survey by the Building Code Committee was presumably derived in the same manner, it is possible to draw at least tentative conclusions as to trends. The Code Committee average of 69.0 pounds shown in Table 23 does not include the same group of cities as does this study. There is some overlapping, however, and the distribution of cities as to size and location is somewhat similar. It is significant to note that the total average and the average for "Seating Not Specified" were approximately 8 pounds less in 1932 than they were in 1922. This indicates that code revision is being attempted on the basis of experimental evidence. The range, however, remains the same, which indicates that revision is being neglected in the situations where the need is most urgent.

In reading, interpreting, and tabulating the load requirements for auditorium floors it was necessary to include in one category all requirements relating to either assembly halls or auditoriums in schools and, in the absence of these individual requirements for schools, to include requirements for assembly halls or auditoriums in general. As in the case of classrooms, there has been a considerable reduction over a ten-year period in requirements for live floor loads in auditoriums with fixed seats. In the case of the auditorium with movable seats or seating not specified, the reduction is not so noticeable. The average, as shown by this study, is 71.5 pounds per square foot for fixed seating, or approximately 20 pounds in excess of the minimum set by the Code Committee.

For floors for office purposes and for rooms with fixed seats, as in churches, school classrooms, reading rooms, museums, art galleries, and theatres, the minimum live load shall be taken as 50 pounds per square foot uniformly distributed.[34]

In the paragraph which immediately follows the above quotation the standard of 100 pounds per square foot is given for corridors, lobbies, stairways, and assembly halls without fixed seats. Reference is not made to any specific type of building, but the intent is to govern the loading in all public buildings. The average live floor load requirement for movable seating in the auditorium in this study was approximately five pounds in excess of that recommended as sufficient by the Code Committee.

The average load requirement when seating is not specified is approximately 100 pounds per square foot. This is only about 4 pounds less than the average of this study for movable seating, and conforms with the recommendations of the Code Committee for movable seating. When loading requirements are written without reference to seating conditions, it may be assumed that the writers intended to provide for the average situation by fixing requirements high enough to meet all possible conditions, including the most extreme loading on a floor without seats. In the absence of definite assurance that fixed seating will not be converted into movable seating to satisfy some future need, this procedure is wholly defensible. It seems, however, that there are two distinct types of school auditoriums or assembly rooms, and that seating conditions for these two types may be determined for the life service of the building. In the first division, for which requirements may be somewhat less, are the auditoriums with large dimensions, sloping floors, and other features which definitely and permanently call for fixed seating. In the second division, for which requirements should be higher, is included the type of room which may be termed a general purpose room. Multiple use requires that minor auditoriums, auditorium-gymnasiums, special activity rooms, and other similar rooms be planned without fixed seating. It would be sound economy and within reasonable safety to draft requirements separately for the two classes of auditoriums.

It is significant to note that while requirements for live loads in classrooms and auditoriums were excessively high, the pro-

[34] Building Code Committee, *op. cit.*, p. 5.

TABLE 24

AVERAGE MINIMUM LIVE LOADS TO BE USED IN CALCULATING THE REQUIRED STRENGTH OF FLOORS IN CORRIDORS, GYMNASIUMS, LABORATORIES, UPPER AND LOWER STORIES, AND STAIRWAYS

(One Hundred Cities of Different Sizes)

	Average Load	Number of Codes	Range
1. Corridors			
Individual requirements for schools	89.9	37	60–100
Blanket requirements for schools	105.9	11	100–120
Total	93.5	48	60–120
U. S. Bureau of Standards Survey	92.5	96	50–150
2. Stairways			
Individual requirements for schools	95.8	23	60–200
Blanket requirements for schools	100.2	23	70–125
Total	98.0	46	60–200
3. Laboratories	80.9	9	60–100
4. Gymnasiums			
Individual requirements for schools	100.0	2	100
Blanket requirements for schools	113.2	19	100–150
Total	111.9	21	100–150
5. Upper Floors	72.4	17	60– 75
6. Lower Floors	86.5	17	60– 90

Note: The U. S. Bureau of Standards reported only on loads for corridor floors. This was given individually for schools.

visions for live loads on corridors and stairways are less on the average than recommended by the Code Committee. Table 24 shows these total averages to be 93.5 pounds per square foot for corridors and 98.0 pounds per square foot for stairways. The apparent reason for these reductions will be considered a little later in the discussion on individual and blanket requirements.

Only nine codes provided for the minimum live load on laboratory floors. The segregation of a laboratory from a classroom is wholly justified on the basis of the type and amount of equipment to be installed. Since no authoritative standards have been made available for this particular type of loading, it is not surprising that codes varied extensively as to requirements.

The average of 111.9 pounds for gymnasiums is in excess of the 100 pounds recommended by the Code Committee. Twenty-one codes recognized the gymnasium as an individual type of room with respect to demands on floor strength.

There were seventeen building codes that specified minimum

live load requirements on the basis of the height of the floor above grade. These requirements, as shown in Table 24, were higher for the ground and lower floors than for the upper floors. No distinction was made between the various types of rooms or the different seating conditions within the rooms. A literal interpretation would apply the average requirement of 72.4 pounds per square foot for upper floors to all areas exclusive of stairways and corridors, irrespective of seating conditions. The averages for both upper and lower floors are considerably in excess of standard requirements for fixed seating, and much lower than would be required for movable seating.

It is difficult to understand the assumptions which imply a heavier loading on the lower floors than on the upper floors of a school. Although no positive evidence has been collected to show a distribution of loading on the various floors of a school, casual observation is enough to show that upper and lower floors are subjected to similar live loads.

Of vital importance from the viewpoint of both economy and structural stability are the implications drawn from the contrasts between individual and blanket requirements for live floor loads for schools. The classroom is exclusively characteristic of the school building; hence all but one code gave individual attention to its loading requirements. In the case of the auditorium, however, there were both individual and blanket requirements for the three types of seating conditions. A total of fifty-three codes made provision for minimum loading on auditorium floors. Twenty-eight of these made individual provisions for the school and twenty-five governed by means of blanket requirements. Seventeen of the codes that specified blanket requirements and three of the codes that specified individual requirements for schools included two requirements each, one for movable and one for fixed seating. It is significant to note that twenty-three of the individual requirements for schools were written without reference to types of seating, and that only seven recognized the need of differentiation in seating. When schools are governed under blanket provisions the situation is reversed. This fact seems to indicate that code writers are more familiar with the demands and characteristics of the general type of public auditorium than they are with the use of the various auditoriums and assemblies within the school.

The difference between the average of 75.0 pounds per square foot for the individual requirements and 70.9 pounds per square foot for blanket requirements, in Column 3 of Table 23, indicates a distinction, in the judgment of code writers, between schools and other buildings. The same conclusion may be drawn from Columns 6 and 9 for movable seating and seating not specified. In the latter column the average for school auditoriums is approximately 13 pounds less than for auditoriums in general. The obvious conclusion is that code writers assumed the occupancy of a school auditorium to be of lighter weight than the occupancy of the general class of auditoriums. To anyone familiar with the frequent community use of the school auditorium, such a distinction is fallacious. In Table 24 reductions are shown again for the school corridor and the stairway, indicating further assumptions that these structural features of the school building require less floor strength than do corridors and stairways in general.

Although the number of cases included in some of the seating classifications for auditoriums are too few to furnish conclusive evidence, the consistency of the evidence throughout indicates an unmistakable tendency to set different minimum floor load requirements for schools. Apparently there has been some effort on the part of code drafters to think of the school as a separate type of building. Closer cooperation between school authorities who administer the educational program and who are familiar with the occupancy of the school under all conditions and code writers would doubtless serve to secure more uniformity, safety, and economy in regulation.

The average requirements of the different groups of cities for classrooms and auditoriums show that the larger cities are more consistent in providing requirements and in setting these requirements at reasonable levels in harmony with authoritative standards. This latter assertion is substantiated by the averages shown for "Seating Not Specified" where a sufficient number of cases are included. In the largest city group, one code, that of Los Angeles, prescribed 75 pounds per square foot for fixed seating in both classrooms and school auditoriums and 125 pounds for movable seating in these two types of rooms. With only four cities included in the largest city group, the high requirements noted for Los Angeles would influence the average to an undue extent. The Los Angeles Code appeared to have a very superior section devoted exclusively to school buildings. Measured by authoritative standards its requirements for live floor loads are excessive, but the otherwise scientific construction of the code leads to the conclusion that there was some defensible reason, such as providing additional lateral strength to withstand the shock of earthquakes.

The true significance of the ranges and averages for minimum live floor load requirements for the various types of school floors is seen in the risks of collapse or failure on the lower levels, and the excessive costs imposed by requirements on the higher levels. Very few requirements approach the danger point, while a very significant number are high enough to increase materially and without justification the cost of floor construction. This additional cost not only is shown in increased quantity or quality of the floor but is reflected in increased quantity or quality of columns, walls, and other vertical supports which bear the additional dead load of the heavier floor. The determination of exact cost differences between the various live load requirements is an expert estimator's problem. An approximation of needless costs, which become considerable in larger schools, is indicated in the following quotation:

> The cost of floor construction is very rapidly increased as the live loads specified are increased. A difference of 125 pounds in the live load means a difference in cost exceeding 50 cents per square foot of floor area. The item of abnormally high live load specifications on schoolhouse floors runs into thousands of dollars of useless expense each year.[35]

The live loads and the dead loads do not comprise the only requirements in the determination of the ultimate strength of floors. In structural engineering and in the legal acts applying thereto it is almost axiomatic to assume, in addition to the specified dead and live loads, a certain factor of safety. This factor ranges from about one and one-half to four or five, and when applied through the required strengths of structural steel, reinforced concrete, or other material it serves to raise the final load-bearing strength to a level which is beyond the possibility of failure or collapse. The intent of the factor of safety is to counterbalance defects in materials, workmanship, and assembly. It is

[35] Stanley Macomber, "The Comprehensive School Building," *National Education Association, Addresses and Proceedings*, p. 639, 1921.

readily seen, therefore, that the initial difference between the cost of a 50-pound live load bearing floor and a 75-pound live load bearing floor is progressively increased as the dead load and the factor of safety are applied.[36]

BEARING WALLS

REQUIRED THICKNESS

Requirements with reference to the minimum thicknesses of the bearing walls of varying types of structures are usually written in such terms as to be intelligible to the average layman, as the following indicates.

Section 80. Thickness of Masonry Walls.

1. All bearing walls shall be of sufficient thickness to support the load to be carried without exceeding the stresses specified in Section 112 but in no case shall such walls be less than the thickness required by Paragraph 3 of this Section, unless built of reinforced concrete.

2. The minimum thickness of all brick bearing walls shall be in accordance with the following schedules. In determining the thickness of walls for varying heights they shall be measured to the nearest tier of beams for support whether this be a foundation of beam or a girder.

3. The expression "walls for the dwelling house class" shall be taken to mean and include walls for all buildings specified under Classes C and D, as well as all other buildings used for temporary residences.

Table indicating minimum thickness of walls in accordance with above requirements:

Stories	1	2	3	4	5	6	7	8	9	10
1*	8									
2*	8	8								
3*	12	8	8							
4	16	12	12	12						
5	16	16	12	12	12					
6	16	16	16	12	12	12				
7	20	16	16	16	12	12	12			
8	20	20	16	16	16	12	12	12		
9	20	20	20	16	16	16	12	12	12	
10	24	20	20	20	16	16	16	12	12	12

* *Note*: Where story height exceeds 12 feet these walls must be twelve inches.

4. The expression "walls for the warehouse class" shall be taken to mean and include walls for all buildings specified under classes A, B, E, and F as well as all other buildings used for similar purposes.

[36] Criticism and advice by courtesy of Messrs. A. L. Stevenson and V. J. Pacello of Elwyn E. Seely & Company, Consulting Engineers, New York City.

Table indicating minimum thickness of walls in accordance with the above requirements:

Stories	1	2	3	4	5	6	7	8	9	10
1	12									
2	12	12								
3	16	12	12 (65 ft.)							
4	16	16	12	12						
5	20	16	16	12	12					
6	24	20	20	16	16	12				
7	24	24	20	20	16	16	12			
8	28	24	24	20	20	16	16	12		
9	28	28	24	24	20	20	16	16	12	
10	32	28	28	24	24	20	20	16	16	12[37]

There is, however, a technical phase of these requirements which deals with the required strength of brick or other units of construction either individually or laid up in masonry, and which takes into account wind pressures, loads, and other factors. It is not the intent of this study to inquire into the engineering aspects of wall construction, but rather to note the various methods employed in regulating the thickness of school building walls, and to raise certain issues concerning those factors which seem to apply especially to schools.

Building codes invariably include requirements similar in form or effect to those quoted above. These requirements are usually followed by qualifying provisions which are intended to control the length or height of unsupported walls and to regulate the proportional amount of openings in walls. Provisions relating to the thicknesses of walls laid up with hollow units, of panel walls, curtain walls, fire walls and parapet walls are usually included.

6. The height of a wall between lateral supports shall not exceed fifteen times its thickness unless strengthened by piers or cross-walls as the Building Inspector may direct.

7. When the clear span of a floor is greater than twenty-five feet in buildings of Classes A, B, E and F and greater than twenty-six feet in buildings in Classes C and D, the thickness of bearing walls shall be increased four inches over that specified in the foregoing sections for every twelve and one-half feet or fraction thereof that said span exceeds twenty-five feet for buildings of Classes A, B, E and F or twenty-six feet for Classes C and D; or shall have in place of this increase of thickness such piers or buttresses as the Building Inspector may direct.

8. Every bearing wall faced with brick laid in running bond shall be four inches thicker than specified in the foregoing sections.

[37] Harrisburg, Pa., *Building Code*, p. 34, 1924.

9. If any horizontal section through a bearing wall shows more than thirty per cent area of flues and openings in a wall laid up in lime, or lime and cement mortar, or forty-five per cent in a wall laid up in Portland cement mortar, the said wall shall be increased a thickness of four inches for every fifteen per cent or fraction thereof for which the total area of flues and openings exceed thirty per cent or forty-five per cent. The total area of openings and flues in any bearing wall shall not in any case exceed sixty per cent.

10. In all buildings, walls eight inches thick and over fifty feet in length, and walls twelve inches thick and over seventy-five feet in length, and walls sixteen inches thick which are over a hundred feet in length, shall be four inches thicker throughout than is required by the preceding sections unless they are braced by cross-walls or buttresses to the satisfaction of the Building Inspector.[38]

Since requirements relating to brick masonry bearing walls included the largest single item in these sections, and since the form and terms of these requirements were readily translated into comparable units, it was decided to use bearing wall requirements for purposes of comparison. The variations among the codes themselves, and the variations between the codes and standard recommendations, are significant, not only in themselves but in the suggestion that similar variations would likely be found if comparisons were made for less conspicuous wall formations.

Table 25 and Chart II show the variations found in the 97 building codes which contained requirements on wall thicknesses. The purpose of Chart II is to show the various thicknesses and combinations of thicknesses prescribed for school building walls of one-, two-, three-, and four-story heights. It should be noted that these variations are increased by the inclusion of basement walls. Twenty codes either lacked provisions for foundation or basement walls or contained provisions that were too vague or general for positive interpretation. Thus, the variations for basement wall thicknesses include only eighty of the codes, but the variations for wall thicknesses above the basement include all the ninety-seven code requirements. In the case of the wall shown at the extreme right, no basement wall thicknesses were given.

In planning the chart, a uniform story height of 14 feet from one floor to the next was assumed. In practice this height may vary, but for purposes of comparison it is as good as any other, since it is well within the story height limits set by any code. In a few instances the thicknesses of walls were specified in the odd

[38] Harrisburg, Pa., *Building Code*, Sec. pp. 34–35, 1924.

TABLE 25

MINIMUM REQUIRED THICKNESS OF BRICK BEARING WALLS[1]

(Expressed in Number of Bricks per Lineal Foot of Wall[2])

	AVERAGE NUMBER OF BRICKS PER LINEAL FOOT OF WALL				
	Number of Codes	One-story Building	Two-story Building	Three-story Building	Four-story Building
Warehouse Class					
0– 10,000......	1	294	588	979	1,370
10,000– 50,000......	10	294	588	979	1,380
50,000–100,000......	7	294	602	958	1,384
100,000–500,000......	9	294	588	968	1,381
Over 500,000......					
TOTAL............	27	294	592	966	1,381
*Miscellaneous Classes**					
0– 10,000......	2	294	588	931	1,370
10,000– 50,000......	20	284	612	979	1,391
50,000–100,000......	21	285	583	960	1,358
100,000–500,000......	21	271	563	919	1,317†
Over 500,000......	3	294	620	979	1,435
TOTAL............	67	281	588	952	1,359
Schools					
0– 10,000......					
10,000– 50,000......	2	294	685	1,076	1,564
50,000–100,000......					
100,000–500,000......					
Over 500,000......	1	294	685	1,076	1,564
TOTAL............	3	294	685	1,076	1,564
Total, All Classes					
0– 10,000......	3	294	588	947	1,370
10,000– 50,000......	32	288	609	982	1,398
50,000–100,000......	28	287	588	959	1,364
100,000–500,000......	30	278	572	934	1,337†
Over 500,000......	4	294	637	1,003	1,467
GRAND TOTAL......	97	285	592	960	1,372
U. S. Bureau of Standards Recommendation‡		294	588	931	1,322

Note 1: In a few codes requirements for wall thicknesses were given in the odd numbers of 9″, 13″, 17″, and 21″. These were included in the calculations as 10″, 12″, 16″, and 20″, respectively.

Note 2: The bases for the calculations were 14-foot story heights with 21 bricks to each square foot.

* Miscellaneous Classes included a number of classifications, such as "Public Buildings," "Business Buildings," "Dwelling House Class," and "Light Duty Buildings."

† One code did not give wall thicknesses above the third story.

‡ Adapted from the Report of the Building Code Committee of the U. S. Bureau of Standards, *Recommended Minimum Requirements for Masonry Wall Construction*, p. 7, 1925.

CHART II

Variations in the Minimum Required Thickness of Brick Bearing Walls, and a Comparison Between These Variations and the Minimum Recommended by the United States Bureau of Standards

(Ninety-seven Code Requirements Taken from Cities of Various Sizes Throughout the United States)

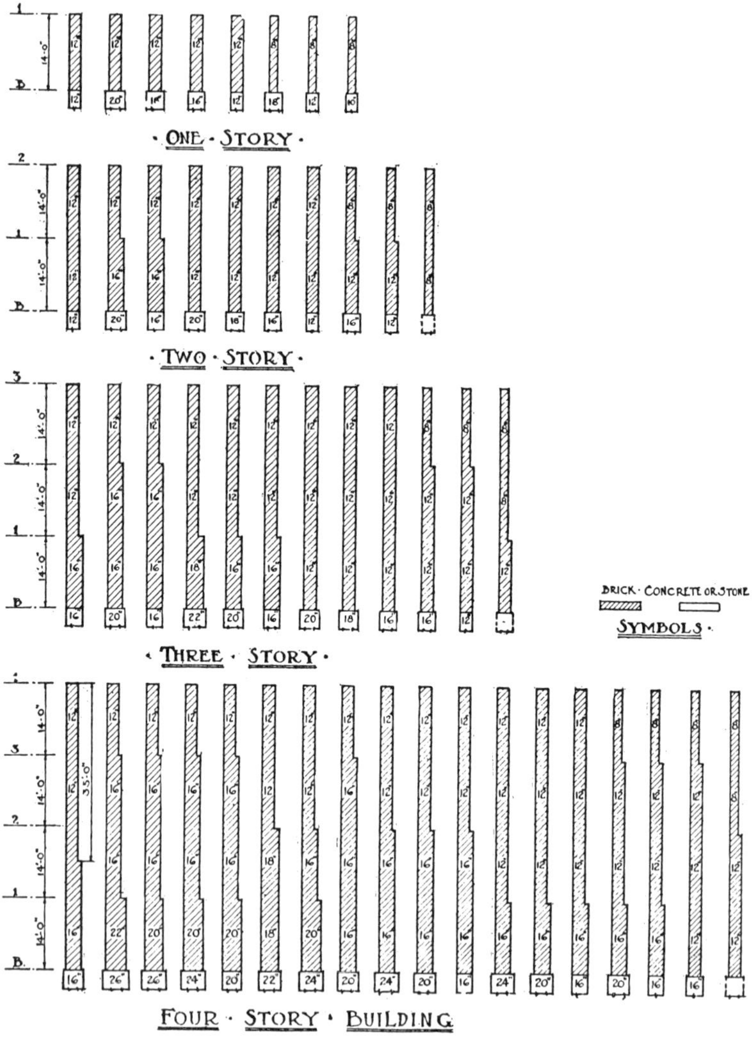

Note 1: The cross section of wall outlined heavily in black at the extreme left represents the U. S. Bureau of Standards Minimum.

Note 2: The cross section of wall for two-, three-, and four-story heights shown at the extreme right was taken from a requirement which was not clear as to the required thicknesses of basement walls.

numbers, 9″, 13″, 17″, and 21″. These thicknesses are adapted to certain variations in size of brick used in different parts of the country, but since they do not involve an increase or decrease in the number of bricks required, they were tabulated as 10″, 12″, 16″, and 20″, respectively. A small number of codes governed the thickness of walls by requiring that the uppermost 35 feet be at least 12 inches thick, and that each successive 35 feet or fraction thereof measured downward from the top of the wall be increased 4 inches in thickness. These requirements, of necessity, had to be interpreted in terms of story heights so that they could be included in the comparisons. In the case of the one- and two-story buildings, the thicknesses were 12 inches throughout. In the case of the three-and four-story buildings the 35-foot limitation fell exactly midway between the floors of the first and second stories and the second and third stories, respectively. The wall requirements usually provide for such situations by indicating that the change in thickness may be made at the floor level nearest the 35-foot limit. Since the selection of a 14-foot story height caused this 35-foot point to fall midway between stories, and since there was a choice to be made, it was arbitrarily decided to increase the wall thickness at the floor level, just above the 35-foot point in one-half of the codes, and to increase the wall thickness at the floor level just below the 35-foot point in the other half of the codes. The results thus obtained are in conformity with actual construction procedure, and the average is in agreement with a literal interpretation of the requirements. The same method was used in calculating the average number of bricks required, as indicated in Table 25.

Including thicknesses of basement walls there are seven different combinations specified for the minimum thicknesses of one-story walls, nine different combinations for two-story walls, eleven different combinations for three-story walls, and seventeen different combinations for four-story walls. An analysis made by the United States Bureau of Standards of the requirements of 134 building codes with respect to the solid exterior walls of dwellings revealed a somewhat similar situation. The Bureau comments in a significant way upon the reason for this great variety of practice.

Among the 134 codes there were 3 different minimum thicknesses prescribed for one-story residential buildings, 4 for two-story dwellings, 8 for three-story dwellings, and no less than 12 different minimum thickness arrangements allowable for the different stories of four-story buildings. Other conditions being equal the thickest four-story wall contained 125 per cent more brick than the thinnest. A similar situation was found to exist in regard to walls of hollow tile and hollow concrete block.

Variation, such as demonstrated above, arises in part from the fact that standards of performance are unequal; that exposures and allowable working stresses vary; and that materials and workmanship differ widely in different localities. It also is due in very large measure to local custom, unchecked by adequate knowledge of construction practice elsewhere, and to slavish copying of other ordinances without due regard for the circumstances attending their adoption. In theory, at least, minimum standards of performance should be uniform, irrespective of location and other conditions, except, perhaps, those due to climate, and when departure is made from minimum standards scientifically determined the reasons for such departure should be carefully considered.[39]

The cross section of wall outlined heavily in black in Chart II represents the minimum safe requirement recommended by the United States Bureau of Standards.

The minimum thickness for solid brick exterior bearing or party walls shall be 12 inches for the uppermost 35 feet of their height, and shall be increased 4 inches for each successive 35 feet or fraction thereof measured downward from the top of the wall; except that the top story exterior bearing wall of a building not exceeding three stories or 40 feet in height, or the wall of a one-story commercial or industrial building may be 8 inches thick, provided that such 8-inch wall does not exceed 12 feet unsupported height and that the roof beams are horizontal; and except that exterior solid brick bearing walls of one and two family dwellings may be 8 inches thick when not more than 30 feet in height. When gable construction is used for such dwellings, an additional 5 feet is permitted to the peak of the gable.[40]

It should be noted that the wall section has been increased in thickness at the 35-foot point. This was done for two reasons: first, because the recommendation of the United States Bureau of Standards was not explicit on the point; and, second, because this procedure was essential since the average for the codes using the same method would call for an increase at the 35-foot point.

Critics of the tentative draft of this report have suggested that the 12-inch thickness provided in Part II, section 5, might extend down to the nearest line of floor beams in case the 35-foot limit fell between floors. The 35-foot height, however, allows space for three fair height stories. A 12-inch wall four stories in height is believed undesirable under the circumstances, and three very high

[39] Building Code Committee, *Recommended Minimum Requirements for Masonry Wall Construction*, p. 24.

[40] *Ibid.*, p. 7.

stories at the top of a building are likewise considered inadvisable. With these restrictions in mind the 35-foot limit without modification is seen to involve no particular hardship.[41]

It is significant that the United States Bureau of Standards [42] recommends a minimum thickness of solid brick, concrete, or coursed stone foundation walls equal to that of the walls next above, but in no case less than 12 inches thick. In only a very few instances did local codes recognize this as standard practice.

In interpreting Chart II it should be borne in mind that the variations revealed are for the minimum or initial thicknesses of bearing walls. If the additional requirements providing for increased widths for walls exceeding a wide variety of unsupported or unbraced lengths and heights were to be considered, the variety of practice would be still greater.

The data in Table 25 were developed in their present form after considerable experimentation. In its original form this table was too detailed both for purposes of printing and for easy and significant comparison. Minimum required wall thicknesses were shown in inches for basements and for the separate stories of the four different buildings. A second form showed the averages and the ranges of these thicknesses, but still lacked a unit of comparison that would be meaningful to the reader. It showed, for instance, that the average minimum required thickness of the first story wall of a two-story building in the Warehouse Class was 12.13 inches, and that the corresponding thickness for the Miscellaneous Class was 12.49 inches. To the technician with a slide rule such data would take on significance in terms of the number of bricks required, but to the average reader they would be intelligible only insofar as they were different. The differences expressed in the number of bricks required for each one-foot length of wall, and the cost of bricks at 2, 3, or 4 cents apiece, however, take on a meaning that can universally and immediately be understood.

The calculations in Table 25 were based upon the same data and the same assumptions as were used in the preparation of Chart II. At first thought a difference of a few bricks between the average minimum number required in the various city groups does not seem significant. Assume, however, a school building with 500

[41] *Ibid.*, p. 42.
[42] *Ibid.*, pp. 18–19.

lineal feet of bearing wall and apply the maximum required thickness for a three-story building, and the result in cost will be $1,450 in excess of the cost of a similar wall constructed according to the recommendations of the United States Bureau of Standards.

The differences between the number of bricks required by the extreme high and low requirements are of still further significance. The highest requirement for the one-story building was 50 per cent more than the lowest requirement; for the two-story building the difference was 74 per cent; for the three-story building the difference was 59 per cent; and for the four-story building the difference was 66 per cent.

The almost universal practice of building codes is to group buildings into two main divisions for purposes of regulating wall thicknesses. One division will contain those buildings which are subjected to heavy duty, such as warehouses. The other division is not so well defined and is usually described by a variety of names such as, "Dwelling House Class," "Public and Business Buildings," "Public Buildings," and "Light Duty Buildings." In three codes the schools were governed by an individual schedule for wall thicknesses. Chicago, Joliet, and Moline—all Illinois cities—used this method. It is likely, although not certain, that the latter two adopted their schedules from Chicago. The object in classifying buildings for the purpose of controlling the strength and thickness of walls is to secure walls of a thickness adequate to support the anticipated loads. Thus, warehouses are obviously the most heavily loaded, public or business buildings come next, and dwelling houses are the least heavily loaded.

The outstanding fact revealed by Table 25 is the diversity of opinion with regard to the loading of a school building. Twenty-seven codes assigned the school to the Warehouse Class, sixty-seven of them assigned it to one or another of the groups included in the table under Miscellaneous Classes, and three treated the school as a separate class of building. The average number of bricks required per lineal foot in the Warehouse Class exceeds the average required in the Miscellaneous Class, for all heights, and the average for the Schools class exceeds by a considerable margin the average for either of the other two classes.

It is possible only to speculate concerning the causes which led code writers to assume such a wide variety of loading conditions for schools. It is probable that in their routine of the day's affairs these men have had occasion to become familiar with the interiors and loading conditions of a number of public buildings, office buildings, and similar structures. However, their opportunities to observe the school intimately are fewer, by reason of the location of the school away from the centers of business, and because of the character of the activity which, as contrasted with other building activities, seldom requires their presence. Whatever the reasons may be, the very diversity of practice indicates conclusively that the function and character of the school as an individual type of building are but imperfectly understood by those who write the laws which govern its physical construction. Careful deliberations, experimentation when necessary, and the close cooperation of technicians, school officials, and legal advisers may be expected to yield results which will effect economy, adaptation, and uniformity.

A close examination of Table 25 will show that there is a distinct tendency toward more reasonable requirements as the cities become larger. This conclusion is drawn from the comparisons of the three groups of cities for which a sufficient number of codes were available. The largest city group, comprising only four cities, included and was unduly influenced by the extremely high requirements of the Chicago and Los Angeles codes. Various reasons for the differences between requirements of the city groups suggest themselves. Revision in the smaller city to keep pace with better practice is probably delayed. The high requirements may reflect in part the intention of the drafters to offset the effects of inferior materials, workmanship, and planning by a greater factor of safety. In either case, possible economies are lost because of the cities' failure to provide modern and reasonable standards and to insist upon adequate and competent supervision of building operations.

USE OF BASEMENT FOR INSTRUCTIONAL PURPOSES

Nine of the one hundred building codes included prohibitions on the use of basements for instructional purposes. These restrictions are significant because they are the exclusive characteristic of those codes which include separate sections for school buildings, and because the situations they seek to control have not as yet been positively designated as coming under the jurisdiction of the police power of the code. The transition from the traditional school with toilets, cloakrooms, and classrooms in the basement to modern standards of school hygiene has not been extensive enough to gain general acceptance or legal force. It is maintained, however, that the protection of immature constitutions from the damp, dark, and poorly ventilated rooms of the typical school basement is well within the intended purpose of the building code, the safeguarding of the health and welfare of the children.

The legal restraints of the nine codes with respect to the use of basement rooms for instructional purposes are commendable and the adoption of these restraints by other codes, with certain revisions, is recommended. The provision copied from the St. Paul, Minnesota, Code is typical of the other eight requirements.

> Classrooms, recitation rooms or study rooms shall not be allowed in basements less than twelve feet in height in the clear nor where the floor is more than three feet below the level of the sidewalk at nearest entrance of buildings, or adjoining grade, nor in basements which are not properly lighted by windows as hereinafter provided.
>
> Gymnasiums shall not be considered as classrooms and may be maintained and constructed in basements when so approved by the Commissioner of Public Buildings.[43]

Although this provision and others like it are a decided recognition of the needs of school children, there is a permissive feature that may destroy in part the intended purpose. The provision allows the floor of a classroom to be three feet below the level of the adjoining grade. If rooms are planned this way, and if windows are included to give the required light and ventilation, the sills will of necessity be so close to the grade that surface dusts and other matter will penetrate between windows and sashes when windows are closed, and practically nullify the beneficial effects of open windows. To give the maximum degree of wholesome environment the floors of all instructional rooms should be at least at grade, and preferably three or four feet above, to give an adequate air space between floors and unexcavated grade below.

Three of the codes recognize, in part, the standard stated in the preceding paragraph, but their discriminations between classrooms of the academic type and rooms used for domestic science and manual training are based upon assumptions which have no basis in fact. No one, either layman or expert, would seriously propose that children who have elected courses in manual training, house-

[43] St. Paul, Minn., *Building Code*, p. 86, 1930.

hold arts, or physical education should be deprived of opportunities to study and grow in an environment equivalent in all respects to that of the upper floors.

It shall be unlawful to construct or maintain any classroom for school purposes in the basement of any school building hereafter erected, except for teaching domestic science, manual training or physical culture, if the floor of such room is below the surface of the surrounding ground on all sides of such rooms.[44]

School building authorities have consistently advised against the housing of any part of the educational program in basement rooms. Nevertheless, municipal building laws tacitly sanction such practice, and the scheduling of classes in basement rooms goes on.

Excavations are expensive to make and the results in terms of educational space are undesirable when basement rooms are planned.[45]

Frequently, large excavations have been made without any apparent purpose in the original planning. Later, when the floors above grade become overcrowded, these unplanned basement areas are pressed into use. The makeshift rooms thus developed are most unsatisfactory from every viewpoint. Had the original investment in excavations, foundations, damp-proofing, drainage, stairways, and other features been put into construction above grade the net result would have been wholly justified both economically and educationally.

The analysis of municipal building codes with respect to the use of basement rooms for instructional purposes gives the unmistakable impression that building legislation either has considered this matter to be without its jurisdiction or it has failed conspicuously to understand the character of the educational activity and the physical needs of growing children.

NATURAL LIGHTING AND VENTILATION

The attention given to natural lighting in the one hundred codes is negligible, and where the school is concerned it is practically nonexistent. Only fourteen of the one hundred codes contained individual provisions for the natural lighting of schoolrooms. Ten of these required the glass area to be not less than one-fifth of the floor area; four of them set the minimum at one-sixth of the

[44] Sioux City, Iowa, *Building Code*, Sec. 243, p. 137, 1921.
[45] N. L. Engelhardt, *School Building Programs in American Cities*, p. 36.

floor area. The total omission of natural lighting requirements from a few of the other eighty-six codes, and the character of the requirements in the remaining codes, made it inadvisable to attempt a tabular analysis. In the case of the latter, the terms of the typical provisions were so wholly unrelated to the obvious needs of the school that their application could not, without a most liberal interpretation, include this type of building. The very limited application of provisions like the one quoted from the New Orleans Code raises the pertinent question of how natural lighting shall be secured in a number of other types of buildings.

> Be it further ordained . . . That in all buildings provided with sleeping quarters, every habitable room shall be provided with a window or windows opening directly upon a street, yard or court; such window or windows having a total opening not less than one-tenth (1/10) the floor area of the room to be ventilated. Utility rooms, such as bathrooms, water closet rooms, storage rooms, etc., when not provided with a window or windows as above specified, shall be provided with adequate artificial ventilation.
>
> The attic of all residence buildings shall be ventilated with louvres at the gables or with roof ventilators.[46]

The significant fact to note in this quotation, which is representative of twoscore or more other codes, is the emphasis upon ventilation. Lighting is mentioned in the sub-caption, but a reading of the terms of the provision fails to reveal any treatment except incidentally. In fenestration, codes appear to subordinate the cause of natural lighting to that of ventilation.

It is not within the scope of this study to explore the field of illuminating engineering. Such an undertaking, desirable and needful as it obviously is, is the task of expert technicians in the related fields of illumination and optics. There are, however, certain long-established standards which, although open to criticism, may be accepted as based upon the best experimental evidence available to date. These are the standards which recommend that glass area be not less than one-fifth of the floor area, and that windows be located so as to minimize glare on the front wall of a classroom. Other more detailed standards require windows to extend to within a fixed distance of floors and ceilings. Considering the immediate and the cumulative effects of both natural and artificial lighting upon the comfort, health, and wel-

[46] City of New Orleans, La., *Building, Electrical, and Plumbing Code*, p. 121, 1929.

fare of individuals, it is surprising indeed that municipal building codes have given so little attention to this phase of public protection. In a number of conferences with engineers who had had experience in the drafting of building laws, the question was raised as to why provisions for lighting and sanitation were so meagre in the average city code. The answers indicated no single or positive reason. Apparently the original purposes of the building code—to insure structural stability and safety from fire—continue to dominate the content of these instruments, to the total or partial exclusion of controls over other aspects of public welfare. Thus, tradition, together with some conflict with the jurisdictions of the sanitary and health codes, has been responsible for the present rather haphazard status of lighting and sanitary regulations in local building codes.

The total lack of regulations in some codes, and the inadequacy of the regulations in other codes as revealed in this study, are confirmed by the findings of a similar investigation by George W. Thomas, who concludes his report with a significant observation on the importance of natural lighting.

> To design buildings for good daylighting is as important as to design them for adequate strength. Vastly more people using a building are subject to abuse of eyesight than may ever possibly be injured due to structural inadequacy. While injuries due to structural failures may be catastrophes for a few, the day-by-day abuse of eyesight is a malignant condition that affects all the occupants of a building sooner or later.
>
> Daylight is an absolute essential to the health and safety of users of buildings and structures, and daylight of proper quantity and quality not only promotes and safeguards public health and safety, but also maintains and enhances property values.[47]

Only eighteen of the one hundred building codes prescribed positive requirements with respect to the number of cubic feet of air per minute per person to be supplied by mechanical means. Table 26 shows the number of cubic feet required for each of the eighteen codes. The number of cities represented is too small to furnish conclusive evidence as to prevalent practice. It is certain however, that code writers have not generally considered the above type of requirement essential to municipal control of building construction. The reason for this may be found in any one

[47] George W. Thomas, "The Status of Natural Lighting in Modern Building Codes." Paper presented before the Silver Anniversary Convention of the Illuminating Engineering Society, Pittsburgh, Pa., October 13–16, 1931.

circumstance or a combination of circumstances. The jurisdiction of sanitary codes, the controversial status of mechanical ventilation, the presence or absence of state laws on ventilation, an emphasis on structural and fire safety, these or other factors may have been responsible for the negligible amount of attention given to ventilation in municipal building codes.

TABLE 26

VENTILATION REQUIREMENTS

(*Number of Cubic Feet per Person to Be Supplied by Mechanical Ventilation*)

POPULATION OF CITIES	AUDITORIUMS AND CLASSROOMS			
	Number of Cubic Feet			
	15	20	25	30
0– 10,000				
10,000– 50,000	2		2	4
50,000–100,000			1	2
100,000–500,000		2	2	2
Over 500,000			1	
TOTAL	2	2	6	8
Individual Provisions for Schools			5	3
Blanket Provisions for Schools	2	2	1	5

The quotation on page 140, taken from the New Orleans Code, illustrates the manner in which ventilation is regulated in the majority of codes. Obviously, such provisions have no relationship to the real or apparent needs of the school.

It is a well-known fact that several states have laws governing the ventilation of various types of buildings. Greenburg,[48] using the data assembled by the New York State Ventilation Commission, shows that in 1925 there were seventeen states without ventilation laws governing schools, that seven had laws of a vague and general character, and that twenty-four had laws on the statute books, twenty of which required 30 cubic feet of air per minute per person.

Reports of investigations ranging from the most exhaustive

[48] L. Greenburg, "Necessity for Change in the Ventilation Laws of the United States," *Heating and Ventilating*, Vol. 23, pp. 49–52, January 1926.

type to tentative inquiries, technical treatments, and articles in trade and professional magazines, and various other literature which appeared during the past decade indicate the unsettled status of mechanical ventilation. Proponents of mechanical ventilation, supported by tradition and probably inspired in certain quarters by a lucrative trade in ventilating installations, have presented a forceful case. On the other side have been those individuals and groups who, observing the vast sums invested in mechanical ventilating equipment, have sought further justification for these expenditures and, as a result of their inquiries, have pronounced the installations of the past a waste of public money. A brief review of both sides of the controversy would only add to the confusion and a detailed and critical evaluation of the issue would take an entire volume.

It is, however, in harmony with sound legislative principle to propose that no mandatory measure which involves a considerable expenditure of public money be enacted until the efficacy of such a measure has been established beyond reasonable doubt.

SUMMARY

The data that have been presented in this chapter indicate certain unmistakable trends and practices in municipal building legislation which influence measurably the cost of school construction, which affect the efficiency and educational fitness of the school, and which bear directly upon the health and safety of school children.

1. The attempt to classify the school with other more or less related buildings, and to govern the construction of school buildings under general requirements, has resulted in loss in building efficiency, excessive costs in construction, and increased hazards to the life and health of the school children.
2. The nature of the educational program, and its demands upon appropriate plant characteristics appear to be but imperfectly understood by those who are responsible for the promulgation of municipal building ordinances.
3. Municipal building ordinances are primarily concerned with protecting the public from the menace to health and welfare which fire and structural failure constitute. Less immediate and spectacular hazards, such as insanitary conditions and inadequate lighting, although probably causing ultimate and

more universal suffering and loss in personal efficiency, are given but slight attention.

4. There is a consistency in the evidence which proves that the smaller cities in general have failed to a greater extent than have the larger cities to revise their building laws in harmony with recent progress in the building industry.
5. Much scientific experimentation remains to be done, especially with respect to the schools' demand upon egress facilities and live floor loadings.
6. Excessive requirements persistently suggest the heavy influence of tradition, imitation, and the political preferment of commercial and manufacturing interests.
7. There are two phases of building legislation which, on the surface, appear to present two separate and unrelated problems. One is concerned with the purely scientific and engineering aspects of construction. It is natural that technicians, on the one hand, have assumed this phase to be the exclusive concern of trained engineers, and that school officials have, on the other hand, been well content to have it so. The other phase is concerned with certain structural features which have an immediate relationship to the educational program, which are more readily understood, and which appear to have a special application to the school. In the first phase may be included the calculations of stresses, loads, pressures, and strains; in the second may be included the calculations of the desirable widths of corridors and stairways, the square feet of floor area per pupil, and similar provisions. The latter are properly the concern of the school official and have been so recognized. The former have not been the intimate concern of the school official and have not been so recognized. It is maintained, however, and it is confirmed by the evidence presented in this section, that the bases upon which stresses, strains, and loadings are calculated can best be studied, analyzed, and supplied by those who are in a position to be familiar with the school, its occupants, and its function. It is proposed, therefore, that in the interests of economy, efficiency, and general welfare school officials be required or invited to participate in the deliberations of code-drafting bodies, and that their experience and knowledge be utilized to a greater extent than has apparently been the practice in the past.

CHAPTER V

CONCLUSIONS AND RECOMMENDATIONS

STATE AND LOCAL BUILDING CODES

State and local building codes exercise varying degrees of duplicating jurisdiction over local school building construction. The multiplicity of reviewing agencies thus created, on both the state and local levels, presents a situation which is needlessly cumbersome, complicated, wasteful of public funds and services, and detrimental to the construction of safe and efficient schools. State building codes, administered by the state educational authorities, appear to have extended their sphere of control so as to insure a maximum of safety and economy in construction and educational adaptability in use. The scope of the police power upon which all local building ordinances depend for authority, however, has definitely limited local jurisdiction to the safeguarding of health and safety. The state in its sovereign power may regulate construction activities in such a manner as to safeguard the interests of localities with respect to economy, appropriateness of design, fitness of interior arrangement, and the safety of school children. Since education is a state function, and since the state possesses the requisite authorities to supervise all the essential phases of school building construction, it appears wholly justifiable to propose that the state gradually assume the responsibility for the control of such construction.

The proposal in the preceding paragraph gains force when the contrasts between the detailed requirements of smaller and larger cities are reviewed. With a consistency that points toward certain conclusions, the evidence shows that the compulsions and the restraints of the codes in larger cities are more in harmony with the standards of school building authorities and the recommendations of recognized standardizing agencies. Practice does not show the wide diversity in the larger city that it does in the smaller city. When the state assumes partial or total responsibility for the control of school building operations, the quality of supervision will be equalized throughout the state, and the smaller city, village, or rural community will not be penalized by reason of its size, financial status, or other condition.

ARRANGEMENT AND METHOD OF CONTROL OF LOCAL BUILDING CODES

Tradition and an economy in production, printing, and administration appear to be jointly responsible for prevalent methods in code arrangement. Buildings are assigned to certain general classes such as "Business Buildings," "Public Buildings," or "Residences." Requirements and restraints are then drawn up to cover, not a single specialized type of building, but a general class. In a few codes, and in the instance of certain structural features, waivers or exceptions are made to provide for the peculiar characteristics of individual types of buildings. Schools are usually classified as "public buildings," and are thus subject to the regulations imposed upon this general class except in codes which include individual provisions.

The general plan outlined above would have much virtue if applied in a logical manner. Even to the novice it must be clear, however, that the present method, implying similar hazards, usage, and occupancy for all public buildings, defeats to a marked degree the legal intent of building legislation. In the case of the school building, this fact was amply demonstrated in the data presented in practically every analysis of this study. In the interests of economy, safety, efficiency, and adaptation, buildings should be assembled in groups on the basis of the expected degree of hazard. This grouping, however, should not remain constant for the various component structural features of a building. Thus, under general requirements for means of egress there should be a grouping of buildings whose demands on egress are similar, and under a general requirement on permissible heights of non-fire-resistive buildings there should be a different grouping. Such a procedure would involve a closer analysis of building characteristics than has been required heretofore; it would also involve greater detail in printing and administration. The ultimate returns to the public in increased economy, safety, convenience, and efficiency, would wholly justify the added costs. The school building, with its peculiar needs and characteristics, is an individual type of structure that cannot, without violence to its avowed purpose, be caused to yield to the requirements set up for any very heterogeneous group of structures. The evidence of this study shows that the general requirements, as opposed to individual requirements, fail to supply the consistency and detail in safety that are demanded by the school. General requirements permit the construction of three-story non-fire-resistive schools as often as they prohibit this practice, while individual requirements, heedful of the standards of school building authorities, insist in 75 per cent of the cases upon fire-resistive construction for three-story schools. The same general contrasts may be observed in the detailed specifications for fire-resistance in corridors, stairways, and basements.

THE LOCAL CODE AND FIRE HAZARDS

The chief purpose of both individual and general requirements is to secure structural stability and safety from fire. The former achieves these purposes to a greater degree than does the latter, but with reference to safety from the hazards of fire there is still much to be desired in both types of requirements. When the six major structural features which are known to be the most important factors in protection from fire were considered, there were only eighty individual requirements covering all six. Seventy-one per cent of these were in agreement with current school building standards, while 29 per cent were below. In contrast to this there were 520 general requirements, 35 per cent of which were in agreement with current school building standards and 65 per cent of which were below. It is clear, therefore, that the recommendations of school building authorities are slow in being adopted by municipal building codes. It may safely be inferred that much of the excellent school construction that has been done during the past decade has gone far beyond the dictates of the local code.

It would seem reasonable to suppose that, as differences in the costs of fire-resistive and non-fire-resistive buildings decrease, there would be justification for the legal compulsion of the safer construction. According to authorities in the field of code drafting, this procedure would likely be held void by the courts since the police power of the local code may not specify a higher type of construction than that consistent with reasonable safety. The question of costs does not enter into the consideration in any way. The standards proposed as a result of this study are, therefore, confined to recommendations for the inclusion in local building codes of all the desirable safety measures which are likely to find legal sanction. These recommendations, although not requiring complete fire-resistance in buildings above one story in height, if adopted would mean the strengthening of practically all the codes included in this study.

THE STATUS OF SANITATION, LIGHTING, AND LOADING

Municipal building legislation is primarily concerned with phases of construction which are designed to secure structural stability and safety from fire. Other aspects of public health, safety, and welfare are included in such a restricted manner as to be practically noneffective in the case of many types of buildings. Thus, provisions for natural and artificial lighting, toilet facilities, and permissible uses of basements in school buildings are totally missing, or so incomplete as to be of little benefit. It seems inconsistent, considering the stated purpose of building legislation, that conditions which may and do cause more far-reaching and universal effects upon health and comfort should be so uncontrolled.

As revealed by this study, there appears to be an urgent need of cooperation between builders, engineers, and school officials in the enactment of school building regulations. Even in those technical phases of construction where only the science of engineering seems capable of operating there is deficiency in information unless the experience and knowledge of the educator are supplied.

NEED OF FURTHER STUDY

The scope of this study was necessarily limited by time and space allotments, but tentative analyses were projected along a number of additional lines, the results of which are not reported herein. Enough data were gathered to indicate that the situations reported in detail in this study would probably be repeated if complete analysis were to be made of requirements governing the construction of school auditoriums, the fireproofing of structural steel and iron, the permissible use of various materials, the construction of roofs and floors, and the arrangement and specifications for plumbing. With respect to the auditoriums there is a decided lack of uniformity of regulation. In only two or three of the modern school codes are there provisions set up specifically for the school. Other codes have not the least reference to the auditorium of the modern school. All the codes, however, have very explicit regulations regarding the construction of theatres and motion picture halls.

During the early part of this investigation an inquiry was sent to the building officials of thirty-eight large cities, with a view to determining the extent to which the theatre sections of the code were interpreted as applying to the school auditorium. Twenty-one replies were received. Seven of them indicated that the practice was to apply theatre regulations to school auditoriums. The other fourteen replies showed that theatre regulations applied in varying degrees, and that numerous waivers, exceptions, and "understandings" are the bases for the regulation of auditorium construction. Any accurate analysis of auditorium regulations would have involved a detailed questionnaire to the building officials of the one hundred cities, and in some instances it would have required a personal interview. Helpful as such an analysis would have been, it had to be abandoned.

Brief investigations of the requirements governing the covering or protection of steel and iron columns, girders, joists, and beams, with brick, terra cotta, or concrete showed that variations in practices and departures from standards are common. At first thought it would appear that this aspect of construction could have no possible significance for the school as an individual type of building. But when requirements for the covering of roof trusses above school auditoriums and gymnasiums are written with varying degrees of severity, these provisions assume special significance. Consider the quotation below which is typical of the more lenient provisions found in building codes.

> The protective covering may be omitted from roof trusses in one-story buildings or where such trusses are over floor areas having a clear height of 20 feet below the bottom chords, provided there is hung immediately below the bottom chords a continuous ceiling of not less than one-hour fire resistive construction.[1]

This requirement makes possible a considerable saving in construction costs when auditoriums, gymnasiums, and other similar spaces are not more than twenty feet in height. In the Chicago code and in a few others which apparently follow Chicago's ex-

[1] Manchester, N. H., *Building Code*, Sec. 313, pp. 138–39, 1930.

ample, coverings must be supplied for *any* height, no savings being possible under any conditions of planning. In other ordinances the height limitations range from 14 to 20 feet, with corresponding degrees of economies made possible. Although wholly tentative, the facts regarding these phases of construction indicate that variations as to practice would be similar to those found in the detailed investigations of this study.

The diversity of practice found in the detailed and tentative investigations of this study suggests the probability of an extension of this condition to a multitude of other items including such matters as the regulation of electrical wiring and installation, of automatic sprinkler systems, and of the use of temporary one-story frame school buildings.

The excessive costs involved in the case of those requirements which are severe beyond reasonable need, and the dangers and inefficiencies resulting from inadequate requirements, indicate beyond doubt a pressing need of the general revision of the form and content of the city building code with respect to those provisions which are directly associated with school building construction.

BIBLIOGRAPHY

ADVISORY COMMITTEE ON ZONING, U. S. BUREAU OF STANDARDS. *A Zoning Primer.* Washington, D. C.

BASSETT, EDWARD M. *Constitutional Limitations on City Planning Powers.* City of New York, Board of Estimate and Apportionment, 1917.

The Building Code, A Symposium. American Institute of Steel Construction, Inc., New York

BUILDING CODE COMMITTEE. *Minimum Live Loads Allowable for Use in Design of Buildings.* U. S. Bureau of Standards, Department of Commerce, Washington, D. C., 1925.

BUILDING CODE COMMITTEE. *Recommended Minimum Requirements for Fire Resistance in Buildings.* U. S. Bureau of Standards, Department of Commerce, Washington, D. C., 1931.

BUILDING CODE COMMITTEE. *Recommended Minimum Requirements for Masonry Wall Construction.* U. S. Bureau of Standards, Department of Commerce, Washington, D. C., 1925.

BURTON, FRANK. "History of Building and Fire Prevention Codes." *National Fire Protection Association Quarterly,* pp. 364–79.

BYRNE, LEE. *Check List Materials for Public School Building Specifications.* Contributions to Education, No. 492. Bureau of Publications, Teachers College, Columbia University, New York, 1931.

CASSEL, ELLWOOD B. "School-Planning for Efficiency and Economy." *The Architectural Record,* August 1932.

CLAY, SIR FELIX. *Modern School Buildings.* B. T. Batsford, Ltd., London, 1929.

COOKE, MORRIS LLEWELLYN. *Our Cities Awake.* Doubleday, Page and Co., New York, 1918.

COOPER, FRANK IRVING. "Standardization of Schoolhouse Planning and Construction." *National Education Association, Addresses and Proceedings,* pp. 568–75, 1918.

DACY, GEORGE H. "Why Not a Nation-Wide Building Code?" *Scientific American,* November 1921.

DOMINGE, C. C. AND LINCOLN, W. O. *Fire Insurance Inspection and Underwriting.* The Spectator Company, New York, 1929.

DOUGHERTY, T. F. AND KEARNEY, P. W. *Fire.* G. P. Putnam's Sons, New York, 1931.

DUFFUS, R. L. *Mastering a Metropolis.* Harper & Brothers, New York, 1930.

"Enforcement of Building Code Provisions." *The American City,* pp. 6–8, January 1923.

ENGELHARDT, N. L. "Modern Ideas for Modern Schools." *The Architectural Forum,* December 1931.

ENGELHARDT, N. L. *Standards for Junior High School Buildings.* Bureau of Publications, Teachers College, Columbia University, New York, 1932.

ENGELHARDT, N. L. *School Building Programs in American Cities.* Bureau of Publications, Teachers College, Columbia University, New York, 1928.

ENGER, E. H. "Test Shows Actual Live Load on School Room Floor." *Engineering News-Record,* May 6, 1920.

ESCOTT, IVAN. "Fire Protection for Schools." *The American School Board Journal,* Vol. 80, p. 68, June 1930.

FERGUSON, JOHN A. "Theory and Practice in Writing Building Laws." *Proceedings of the Engineers' Society of Western Pennsylvania,* Vol. 30, February 1914.

FITZ-ELWYNE'S ASSIZ OF BUILDINGS, I RICHARD I (1189). "The Pioneer Building Ordinance." *National Municipal Review Supplement,* Vol. 17, pp. 555–63, 1928.

FITZPATRICK, F. W. *Building Code.* American School of Correspondence, Chicago, 1913.

FLEMING, ALFRED T. "Is Your School a Fire Trap?" Reprinted with permission of *The Ladies' Home Journal* by National Board of Fire Underwriters, New York, 1932.

FORESTER, H. W. "Fire Protection for the Schools." *The American Architect,* Vol. 117, Pt. III, March 10, 1920.

FREEMAN, FRANK N. "Illumination Requirements of School Buildings." *National Education Association, Addresses and Proceedings,* pp. 339–53, 1919.

FREITAG, J. K. *Fire Prevention and Fire Protection.* John Wiley & Sons, New York, 1921.

FREUND, ERNST. *Police Power.* Callaghan & Co., Chicago, 1904.

FREUND, ERNST. *Administrative Power over Persons and Property.* University of Chicago Press, Chicago, 1928.

GAMBLE, S. G. *A Practical Treatise on Outbreaks of Fire.* J. B. Lippincott Company, Philadelphia, 1926.

GREENBURG, L. "Necessity for Change in the Ventilation Laws of the United States." *Heating and Ventilating,* Vol. 23, January 1926.

HARPER, ROBERT FRANCIS. *The Code of Hammurabi.* University of Chicago Press, Chicago, 1904.

HART, FRANK W. *A Standard State Schoolhousing Code.* C. F. Williams & Son, Albany, 1924.

ITTNER, WILLIAM B. "Standardization of School Buildings." *National Education Association, Addresses and Proceedings,* pp. 375–79, 1917.

LAIRD, DONALD A. "School Noises and How to Minimize Them." *The Nation's Schools,* Vol. 3, January 1929.

MACOMBER, STANLEY, "The Comprehensive School Building." *National Education Association, Addresses and Proceedings,* pp. 638–40, 1921.

MCCORNACK, W. R. "School Buildings as They Are and as They Should Be." *National Education Association, Addresses and Proceedings,* pp. 361–64, 1919.

MCGOWAN, H. M. *An Analysis of State School Building Codes of the United States.* Unpublished doctor's dissertation, The Ohio State University, 1929.

MCGOWAN, H. M. "An Analysis of State School Building Codes." *Educational Research Bulletin,* Vol. X, No. 17, November 1931. College of Education, The Ohio State University.

NATIONAL BOARD OF FIRE UNDERWRITERS. "Consider the School-House." *Safeguarding America Against Fire*, Vol. 8, No. 2, February 1925.

NATIONAL FIRE PROTECTION ASSOCIATION. *Building Exits Code.* Boston, 1929.

New York Times, January 15, 1932.

POLLARD, W. L. "Outline of the Law of Zoning in the United States." *Annals of the American Academy of Political and Social Science*, Vol. 55, May 1931.

PROCTOR, A. M. *Safeguarding the School Board's Purchase of Architects' Working Drawings.* Contributions to Education, No. 474. Bureau of Publications, Teachers College, Columbia University, New York, 1931.

Report of the Survey of the Schools of Watertown, Massachusetts. Bureau of Publications, Teachers College, Columbia University, New York, 1931.

Report of the Faneuil Hall Committee. The Fire Prevention Commission of Massachusetts, Boston, 1916.

ROBERTS, H. C. "Fire and Other Insurance for Public School Property." *Proceedings of the Nineteenth Annual Meeting of the National Association of Public School Business Officials*, 1930.

RUSCH, HENRI. "Building Laws." *Journal of the Association of Engineering Societies*, Vol. 53, November 1924.

SALIERS, EARL A. *Depreciation—Principles and Practices.* The Ronald Press Company, New York, 1922.

SCHERER, FRANCIS R. "Comparative Costs of School Buildings at Rochester." *The American School Board Journal*, Vol. 68, February 1924.

School Buildings, Equipment, and Grounds. Bulletin No. 52, Department of Public Instruction, Lansing, Mich., 1922.

School Fires. Bulletin of National Fire Protection Association, Boston, 1931.

SCHWARTZ, H. M. *Improvement in the Maintenance of Public School Buildings.* Contributions to Education, No. 240. Bureau of Publications, Teachers College, Columbia University, New York, 1926.

STINEMAN, NORMAN M. "Excessive Floor Loads Specified for School Buildings." *American Architect*, Vol. 123, pp. 334–35, April 11, 1923.

STRAYER, GEORGE D., AND ENGELHARDT, N. L. *Standards for Elementary School Buildings.* Bureau of Publications, Teachers College, Columbia University, New York, 1923.

STRAYER, GEORGE D. AND ENGELHARDT, N. L. *School Building Problems.* Bureau of Publications, Teachers College, Columbia University, New York, 1927.

STRAYER, George D. AND HAIG, R. M. *Financing Education in the State of New York.* The Macmillan Company, New York, 1924.

THOMAS, GEORGE W. "The Status of Natural Lighting in Modern Building Codes." Paper presented before the Silver Anniversary Convention of the Illuminating Engineering Society, Pittsburgh, Pa., October 13–16, 1931.

THOMPSON, GEORGE N. *The Preparation and Revision of Local Building Codes.* Municipal Administration Service, Publication No. 2, New York, 1927.

WOMRATH, G. F. *Efficient Business Administration of Public Schools.* The Bruce Publishing Company, Milwaukee, 1932.